THE
IMPORTANCE
AND VALUE
OF PROPER
BIBLE STUDY

Register This New Book

Benefits of Registering*

- ✓ FREE **replacements** of lost or damaged books

- ✓ FREE **audiobook** – *Pilgrim's Progress*, audiobook edition

- ✓ FREE information about new titles and other **freebies**

www.anekopress.com/new-book-registration

*See our website for requirements and limitations.

THE
IMPORTANCE
AND VALUE
OF PROPER
BIBLE STUDY

HOW TO PROPERLY STUDY
AND INTERPRET THE BIBLE

REUBEN A. TORREY

We love hearing from our readers. Please contact us at www.anekopress.com/questions-comments with any questions, comments, or suggestions.

The Importance and Value of Proper Bible Study

© 2021 by Reuben A. Torrey

All rights reserved. First edition 1921.

Revisions copyright 2021.

Cover Designer: Jonathan Lewis

Editors: Sheila Wilkinson and Ruth Clark

Aneko Press

www.anekopress.com

Aneko Press, Life Sentence Publishing, and our logos are trademarks of Life Sentence Publishing, Inc.
203 E. Birch Street
P.O. Box 652
Abbotsford, WI 54405

RELIGION / Christian Living / Spiritual Growth

Paperback ISBN: 978-1-62245-790-8

eBook ISBN: 978-1-62245-791-5

10 9 8 7 6 5 4 3 2

Available where books are sold

Contents

Introduction

There is a great and constantly growing interest in the study of the English Bible in these days. But much of the so-called study of the English Bible is unintelligent and not fit to produce the most satisfactory results. I already have a book entitled *How to Study the Bible for Greatest Profit,*[1] but that book is intended for those who have much time to put into thorough Bible study.

The present book is intended first to impress men with the importance and value of Bible study; secondly, to show busy men how to get the most out of their Bible study; and thirdly, to set forth the fundamental principles of correct biblical interpretation.

The book really consists of four sermons delivered to the members of my own church and congregation in Los Angeles. There were not a few children in the congregation, but they were all interested, long as the

---

1   Republished as *How to Study the Bible Intentionally* by Aneko Press

sermons were, and they seemed to grasp the main points of the sermons. So I am confident this book will be helpful even to those who only have a little education. Some in the congregation who are in an education profession, both secular and religious, have expressed their appreciation of the help received from the sermons.

If one desires to go into the subject more thoroughly, I suggest that he secure my book already mentioned, *How to Study the Bible for Greatest Profit*. This book will probably be followed soon by one on the most fruitful methods of thorough Bible study.

R. A. Torrey

Chapter 1

The Importance and Value of Bible Study

Blessed is the man that walketh not in the counsel of the ungodly, nor standeth in the way of sinners, nor sitteth in the seat of the scornful. But his delight is in the law of the LORD; *and in his law doth he meditate day and night. And he shall be like a tree planted by the rivers of water, that bringeth forth his fruit in his season; his leaf also shall not wither; and whatsoever he doeth shall prosper.* (Psalm 1:1-3)

Our subject first is the importance and value of Bible study. You will find the text in Psalm 1:1-3: *Blessed is the man that walketh not in the counsel of the ungodly, nor standeth in the way of sinners, nor sitteth in the seat of the scornful. But his delight is in the law of the LORD; and in his law doth he meditate day and night. And he shall be like a tree planted by the rivers of water, that bringeth forth his fruit in his season; his leaf also shall not wither; and whatsoever he doeth shall prosper.*

There has perhaps never been an age that set such great store in study as that in which we now live. The unfortunate thing about it is that so much of the study in our day, both by children and adults, is devoted to books and subjects in which there is little or no profit. A large portion of every year in our schools and colleges is practically wasted. Time is squandered on the purely speculative, the uncertain, the unprofitable, the unessential, the unproductive, the irrelevant, and the transitory. Many practical businessmen think that the sooner the boy or girl who recently graduated from school or college forgets half of what they imagine they have learned, the better. The most profitable of all study is wisely ordered Bible study. Its value is incalculable. It is beyond all comparison more profitable than any other study. It is the one superlatively profitable study.

Possibly some of you may be inclined to question that statement, so I will give you two reasons why Bible study is the one superlatively profitable study, why Bible study towers far above all other studies in importance and value.

Because of What the Bible Is

Bible study towers far above all other studies in importance and value because of what the Bible itself is.

In the first place, the Bible is the unequaled masterpiece of clear, pure, clean, forceful, beautiful, exalted English. Nothing can match it in purity, smoothness, clearness, force, and magnificence of expression. That allows no question. All intelligent, well-read, and candid infidels acknowledge that. Professor Phelps at the head of the English department at Yale contended some years ago that candidates for admission to American universities should have their qualification for admission, as far as their knowledge of English was concerned, tested by one book alone – the Bible. And Harvard University has announced in the past few weeks that hereafter every student before graduation must pass an examination in the English Bible. Because of Harvard's well-known theological position, and from the fact that they seem to emphasize the Revised Version, it is evident that they view the Bible as the great English masterpiece.[2]

Last Tuesday I received a book for examination from G. P. Putnam's Sons of New York and London – a dictionary of six thousand choice and effective phrases.

2   Keep in mind that this book is based on a series of messages given in the early 1900's and that sadly, the theological stance of these institutions has since changed drastically.

In this book, time and again, page after page, every phrase was taken from the Bible without variation or addition. Here and there were scattered phrases taken from Shakespeare, but on subject after subject, whole pages of significant phrases were taken from the Bible. Why? Because this book of phrases was prepared by a master of English articulation, and he knew where to find the most illuminating and most telling phrases. Every man and woman should saturate themselves with the very words of the Bible if for no other reason than to clarify, strengthen, and invigorate their English articulation.

When Henry Stanley, the great newspaper writer, made his second tour of exploration into the heart of Africa, he took only one book with him – the Bible. He devoted and improved many lonely hours in his study, and when he emerged, after having been shut up with one book for so many years, it was noticed that Henry Stanley had acquired by absorption an entirely new English style, a far more forceful style – Bible English.

It is said that a newspaper report of a paragraph from one of Mr. Moody's sermons was handed to Max Müller, the great philologist, and he was asked what he thought of it. He asked, "Who wrote that?"

And the reply was made, "D. L. Moody."

"I do not wonder, then, at his power," Max Müller

exclaimed. "That is one of the finest pieces of clear, strong, pure Anglo-Saxon I have ever read." But where had Mr. Moody learned this vigorous English? From the only book he thoroughly knew and daily devoured – the Bible.

Secondly, the Bible is the book that presents the most profound, the most coherent, the most consistent, the most comprehensive, the most complete, the most perfectly balanced, the most certain, the loftiest, and the most enduring system of philosophy ever discovered. I say *discovered* instead of *devised,* for man could have never devised the philosophy found in this Book; man simply discovered the philosophy that God had revealed in the Book. Time and again through the centuries, men who grew wise in their own conceit and had only a ludicrously fragmentary knowledge of the Book upon which they ventured judgment, have determined to ridicule the Bible's philosophy regarding God, man, redemption, duty, and eternity. But always in the ultimate outcome, the philosophy of the would-be critics has dissolved and disappeared, while the philosophy of the Bible has stood unscathed in the storms of centuries. Philosophies, empires, and schools of thought have passed away, but the words of this Book have not passed away (Matthew 24:35). The philosophy of this Book has proven imperishable and as good for AD 1921 as for AD 95.

In view of this undeniable fact, is it not evident that this is the most important and valuable of all books to study? Don't waste your time studying the soap bubbles of man's iridescent speculation that may be beautiful, but soon burst and leave nothing but a nasty, dank, greasy feeling behind. Study the eternal Rock of this Book that is rich with real gold.

In the third place, the Bible is the book that offers us the purest, loftiest, most complete, and absolutely dependable system of ethics ever known. Systems of moral philosophy have appeared throughout the centuries, from Zeno to Herbert Spencer, only to disappear; but after thorough and complete righteousness, all honest seekers bow to the imperishable durability of the ethics of the Bible. And even those who clamor hysterically for us to give up the virgin birth of our Lord, the resurrection of His body from the dead, all His miracles, the deity of our Lord, His atoning, substitutionary death, and other distinctive, doctrinal teachings of the Book nevertheless cry, "Let us keep the ethics of the Bible. They are not only unsurpassed but also absolutely unequaled." The most important thing to know is how to live, not how to live physically but how to live morally. If that is so, then the most important book for all of us to know is the Book that tells us how to live morally, for no other book tells us this.

In the fourth place, the Bible is the one and only book that has never been outgrown or superseded. I had an opportunity last summer, while packing up our home in Montrose, Pennsylvania, to review some of the books I had studied. Yes, I had dug into these for many hard hours of intellectual toil at preparatory school and at Yale. There was not one of them of any present value to my children or grandchildren. They had all been outgrown or superseded; other books have taken their place.

But this Book has not been superseded. No university professor on earth can suggest some other book to take the place of this Book. Some venture to say, "We need a new Bible," but where is it? Why don't they bring it out? When an especially immature and therefore daring member of this crew does attempt a new Bible, it is only "a shorter Bible," that is, the old Bible with parts left out that made him uneasy in his sin or in his self-righteousness and self-sufficiency. No! No! NO! Anyone who has an iota of real, healthy common sense knows that you cannot outgrow or supersede the Bible. And we can safely leave those who want to get "a new Bible" to sit and twiddle their thumbs along with the other lunatics who are working on a perpetual motion machine.

This all being true, and centuries of unvarying history of human thought demonstrate that it is true, can there possibly be any other study so important and so permanently profitable as the study of this, the one and only imperishable Book?

Once more, the Bible is the Word of God. That needs no demonstration. Some of the things I have already said prove it, if you think them through. And I have proven it again and again from this platform. Other books tell us what men suppose; the Bible tells us what God knows. Other books tell us what other men, almost as foolish as ourselves, speculate; this Book tells us what an infinitely wise God, who made us and all things and knows all things, has inerrantly revealed.

If you had two books on a subject, one by the one master thinker on that subject and the other by a third-rate tutor in a fourth-rate college, which would you study most? And will you study most the Book of God, the Book of the infinitely wise, omniscient God, or the book of some little six-by-nine-inch human brain?

Because of What the Bible Does

Bible study towers above all other studies in importance and value not only because of what the Bible is, but also because of what the Bible does.

On this I cannot dwell as I would like. The full exposition of this line of thought would provide more than enough material for a whole sermon by itself. Let me select a few of the more vital points.

First of all, the Bible properly studied makes men wise unto salvation. Paul, the great master apostle, wrote to a zealous young bishop, his convert and most trusted coworker, and said, *But evil men and seducers shall wax worse and worse, deceiving, and being deceived. But continue thou in the things which thou hast learned and hast been assured of, knowing of whom thou hast learned them; and that from a child thou hast known the holy scriptures, which are able to make thee wise unto salvation through faith which is in Christ Jesus* (2 Timothy 3:13-15). This is a tremendous endorsement of the superlative importance of Bible study, and every word of it is true.

This Book does make men wise with the wisdom that is golden, the wisdom that brings eternal salvation. No other book in all literature does it with the certainty and clarity and completeness with which this Book does it. No one can study this Book correctly, no matter how ignorant he may otherwise be, without becoming possessed of that priceless wisdom that means eternal life. Eternal life is found in knowing God and His Son, Jesus Christ (John 17:3). And no other book has the power to make us acquainted with God and with His Son, Jesus Christ, that this Book has.

I have known great philosophers and great men of science and great literary luminaries who did not know God, simply because they had not studied and, therefore, did not know their Bibles. They knew rocks and flowers and the internal parts of frogs; they knew the planets, the comets, the stars, and men's books, but they did not know the one Book. Therefore, they did not know the God who made the rocks and the flowers and the stars. Therefore, they were lost, eternally lost, in spite of all their knowledge of other things.

On the other hand, I have known uncultured people, almost illiterate people, washerwomen and others, who had studied and, therefore, did know the Bible. They knew more of the wisdom that really counts, the wisdom that spells salvation in five minutes, than these learned professors knew in their whole lifetime. Oh, study the Book that brings eternal life, make it in your own experience *the implanted word, which is able to save your souls* (James 1:21 RV).

In the second place, the Bible makes Jesus Christ known so as to lead anyone who studies it to believe in Jesus as the Christ, the Son of God, and thereby to obtain eternal life in His name. That is what John says in John 20:31: *These are written, that ye might believe that Jesus is the Christ, the Son of God; and that believing ye might have life through his name.* Is there anything in all the world so valuable as eternal life? Is there any other study for one moment comparable in importance and value to the study that brings us eternal life?

In former years, I had hay fever severely. Every September for three weeks or more I could not lie down to sleep or even stay in the house at night. I would go off by myself every night where I would not disturb anyone, and all the night long, I would almost rupture blood vessels by spasms of coughing. I saw an advertisement for a book on hay fever, so I bought it and studied it with great care and obtained great relief. Wasn't that profitable study? But what is getting deliverance from such a wretched complaint as hay fever compared to getting eternal life? And the proper study of this Book brings eternal life. No man can study even one book in the Bible, the Gospel of John, in the way he ought to study it, without believing before he gets through it *that Jesus is the Christ, the Son of God,* and by believing, obtaining eternal life in His name (John 20:31). I have proven this repeatedly with all classes of men from bartenders to a college dean in one prominent British university and a very distinguished professor in another.

In the third place, the Bible imparts God's own nature to the men, women, and children who study it as they should and thus completely transforms their inmost and their outward life. Peter puts it this way: through the *exceeding great and precious promises [of the Book]: . . . ye might be partakers of the divine nature* (2 Peter 1:4). Isn't that great – to become a partaker of God's own nature? Well, it is through the proper study of this Book, by the truth of this Book carried home to our hearts by the Holy Spirit as we study it, that we become partakers of God's own nature. Centuries of experience prove the truth of this wonderful assertion by Peter. Countless men and women of the most depraved nature have obtained an entirely new nature, God's own nature implanted in them, by the proper study of this Book.

I have been told that if you study Mrs. Mary Baker Eddy's *Science and Health* persistently, it will cure you of appendicitis. Well, study this Book as you ought, and it will cure you of devilitis. I have found it so in my own experience. Neither Mrs. Eddy nor Christian Science cured me, but this Book did. Try it for yourself.

In the fourth place, when properly studied, this Book makes the one who studies it grow *like the palm tree* in all the graces and glories of Christian character. As Peter says, *Desire the sincere milk of the word, that ye may grow thereby* (1 Peter 2:2). Various neighbors of mine in South Pasadena have built homes since I located there and have set out various kinds of palm trees. It is simply amazing how they have grown. Ah, but that is nothing compared to the way men, women, and children grow spiritually and morally when they feed as they ought to on the *bread of heaven,* the "milk" of Eden, *the finest of the wheat* in the garden of God, and *the honey out of the [eternal] Rock* found in this Book.

Oh, sometimes I almost grow weary when people come moaning to me from the Atlantic to the Pacific, and from the Gulf of Mexico to the border of Canada and beyond, blubbering over their poor progress in the Christian life and wondering why they do not make more headway. And when I ask, "Do you meditate on God's Word day and night? Do you really dig into the Bible every day?" they reply, "Oh no, not every day. I am very busy. I am a very hard-working man," or "I am a very active businessman with many other men under me," or "I am a very busy mother, and I cannot find time to get down to solid Bible study *every* day." So I ask, "Do you read the newspaper every day?" and they respond, "Yes, morning and evening." And yet no time to get alone each day and listen to God?

In the fifth place, the Bible properly studied makes the heart pure and keeps the life white. *Wherewithal shall a young man cleanse his way?* the psalmist asks, and then replies, *by taking heed thereto according to thy word* (Psalm 119:9). There is a power in this Book, when it is properly studied, to make and keep the life clean that no other book possesses. And there is also a power in this Book, when properly studied, that no other book possesses to make and keep the heart pure. The psalmist says again two verses later in Psalm 119:11, *Thy word have I hid in mine heart, that I might not sin against thee.* Oh, how many stained lives I have seen bleached white by the power of the sunrays of this Book. How many hearts I have known that were *full of all uncleanness* to be made pure and clean by filling them with the truth found in this Book.

In the sixth place, the Bible, properly studied, brings

peace, wonderful peace, to the troubled heart. The psalmist says, *I will hear what God the* LORD *will speak: for he will speak peace unto his people, and to his saints* (Psalm 85:8). The one who learns to sit and listen to God as He speaks to him in this Book will hear Him speaking words that will fill his heart with peace, no matter how storms may rage around him and no matter how war howls and bellows. Listening to God's Word, David sang in the midst of the wildest conflicts, *The* LORD *is my light and my salvation; whom shall I fear? the* LORD *is the strength of my life; of whom shall I be afraid? When the wicked, even mine enemies and my foes, came upon me to eat up my flesh, they stumbled and fell. Though an host should encamp against me, my heart shall not fear: though war should rise against me, in this will I be confident* (Psalm 27:1-3).

And just before the wild storm clouds broke in the worst night the disciples ever passed through, in speaking of the peace-giving power of His words, the Lord Jesus said, *But the Comforter, which is the Holy Spirit, whom the Father will send in my name, he shall teach you all things, and bring all things to your remembrance, whatsoever I have said unto you. Peace I leave with you, my peace I give unto you: not as the world giveth, give I unto you. Let not your heart be troubled, neither let it be afraid* (John 14:26-27).

Here is the practical secret of perfect peace – listening to the Savior's words as found in this Book. He is always saying to the wind-driven heart, as He said to the wind-tossed sea of old, *Peace, be still.* And if we listen, there is always *a great calm* (Mark 4:39).

In the seventh place, the Bible, properly studied, brings joy as well as peace. Jeremiah discovered that truth many, many centuries ago. In the midst of crushing sorrow, in the midst of the disintegration and shame and agony of the nation he passionately loved and for which he would gladly have died, in the midst of conditions as dark and foreboding as ever confronted any man on earth, he sang, *Thy words were found, and I did eat them; and thy word was unto me the joy and rejoicing of mine heart* (Jeremiah 15:16). Is there any joy purer than that which comes from properly directed study? But there is no other study that brings joy for a moment comparable to the joy that comes from proper Bible study. Many forms of study bring great joy to a healthy mind. The joys that come from earnest study of various kinds – philosophical, scientific, historical, literary, and linguistic – have been among my chief joys for many years, nearly my whole life from early boyhood. But there has come into my heart a joy from Bible study by digging into the gold mines of this wonderful and inexhaustible Book. But the joys that have come from all other forms of study are not worthy to be compared to this joy for one moment. There are no other joys like this. *Blessed is the man that walketh not in the counsel of the ungodly, nor standeth in the way of sinners, nor sitteth in the seat of the scornful. But his delight is in the law of the Lord; and in his law doth he meditate day and night. And he shall be like a tree planted by the rivers of water, that bringeth forth his fruit in his season; his leaf also shall not wither; and whatsoever he doeth shall prosper* (Psalm 1:1-3).

I might go on and on, telling the great things that the right kind of Bible study will accomplish. There is no end to the subject, so we may as well stop here.

Isn't it as clear as day that the study of a book that is what this Book most assuredly is, and a book that does what this Book most assuredly does, is infinitely the most important and valuable study in the world? The luster of all other study grows dim compared with this. Will you then begin to study the Bible as you ought? Begin today. Please note that I have been careful to say over and over again, "the Bible *properly* studied," that is, the Bible studied in the way and by the methods in and by which it should be studied – studied in a way appropriate to the unique and divine character of the Book. There is Bible study, or at least what is called "Bible study," that is not so profitable as this. Indeed, there is Bible study that is not profitable at all, and even Bible study that is positively injurious. I would rather have a son or daughter of mine study almost anything else than have them study the Bible as they study it at the University of Chicago or in the American Institute of Sacred Literature or in many other places in these days.

I will speak next on how to properly study the Bible: for light and not for darkness, for life and not for death, for blessing and not for cursing, and so it will lift us up to heaven and not sink us down to hell.

Chapter 2

How to Properly
Study the Bible

*These were more noble than those in
Thessalonica, in that they received the word
with all readiness of mind, and searched the
scriptures daily, whether those things were so.*
(Acts 17:11)

M y subject now is how to properly study the
Bible. I have eleven texts in which God Himself
tells us plainly and fully how to study His Book.

Acts 17:11: *These were more noble than those
in Thessalonica, in that they received the
word with all readiness of mind, and searched
the scriptures daily, whether those things were
so.*

Isaiah 8:20: *To the law and to the testimony: if they speak not according to this word, it is because there is no light in them.*

Psalm 1:1-3: *Blessed is the man that walketh not in the counsel of the ungodly, nor standeth in the way of sinners, nor sitteth in the seat of the scornful. But his delight is in the law of the LORD; and in his law doth he meditate day and night. And he shall be like a tree planted by the rivers of water, that bringeth forth his fruit in his season; his leaf also shall not wither; and whatsoever he doeth shall prosper.*

Psalm 119:11: *Thy word have I hid in mine heart, that I might not sin against thee.*

1 Thessalonians 2:13: *For this cause also thank we God without ceasing, because, when ye received the word of God which ye heard of us, ye received it not as the word of men, but as it is in truth, the word of God, which effectually worketh also in you that believe.*

John 7:17: *If any man will do his will, he shall*

know of the doctrine, whether it be of God, or whether I speak of myself.

James 1:22: *But be ye doers of the word, and not hearers only, deceiving your own selves.*

1 Corinthians 2:14: *But the natural man receiveth not the things of the Spirit of God: for they are foolishness unto him: neither can he know them, because they are spiritually discerned.*

Psalm 119:18: *Open thou mine eyes, that I may behold wondrous things out of thy law.*

Matthew 11:25: *At that time Jesus answered and said, I thank thee, O Father, Lord of heaven and earth, because thou hast hid these things from the wise and prudent, and hast revealed them unto babes.*

Luke 24:27: *And beginning at Moses and all the prophets, he expounded unto them in all the scriptures the things concerning himself.*

We saw something of the importance and value of

properly conducted Bible study. We saw that properly conducted Bible study was the one superlatively important study for young and old. We saw that Bible study towered above all other studies in importance and value. But we also saw that not all Bible study had this great importance. We saw that there was much in our day that was called "Bible study" that was not profitable at all; indeed, there was much that was called "Bible study" that was positively injurious.

So our subject now is how to *properly* study the Bible. I use the word *properly* in its exact sense of *appropriately* or *fittingly*. A proper study of the Bible is a study of the Bible that fits the book you are studying. A study of other books that would be perfectly proper for them would not be proper at all for the Bible, for the Bible is what no other book in the world is; the Bible is God's Book and other books are men's books. As Paul said in writing to the believers in Thessalonica, *For this cause also thank we God without ceasing, because, when ye received the word of God which ye heard of us, ye received it not as the word of men, but as it is in truth, the word of God, which effectually worketh also in you that believe* (1 Thessalonians 2:13).

The proper study of the Bible will be the most highly profitable study of the Bible. The improper study of the Bible will be an unprofitable study of the Bible.

The great reason that the kind of study of the Bible as done at the University of Chicago, in the American Institute of Sacred Literature, and in many such places and institutions is so unprofitable and often so positively pernicious and injurious, is that it is so utterly improper and unbefitting the Book upon which it is entrusted. No really intelligent man would study a fairy tale in the same way he would study an accurate and entirely reliable history. And at the University of Chicago they study the histories of the Bible, which are the most exact, accurate, and reliable histories ever written, as if they were fairy tales or folklore. No really intelligent or rational man or woman would study an omniscient God's Word as they would study ever-erring man's word. The Bible is God's Word, and they study it at the University of Chicago as if it were the word of men who did not know quite as much as the very self-sufficient teachers at the University of Chicago know. And that is a very improper, yes, a very foolish way to study the Book that is so clearly demonstrated by eighteen centuries of investigation and uniform experience to be the very Word of God.

How shall we study the Bible so as to study it properly and, therefore, study it for the highest profit? God Himself tells us and He tells us in the Bible itself.

Study the Bible, the Bible Itself

In the first place, study the Bible, the Bible Itself. The importance of that comes out in a very striking way in Acts 17:11: *These were more noble than those in Thessalonica, in that they received the word with all readiness of mind, and searched the scriptures daily, whether those things were so.* Notice, please, that it says they *searched the scriptures daily, whether those things were so.* They did not search the Talmud nor the Targums, the commentaries on the Scriptures; they went right to the Scriptures themselves. They left the muddy streams of man's interpretations of the Scriptures and went to the pure, crystal spring – the Scriptures themselves. That is the proper way to study the Bible, as it is God's Word. And as it alone is God's Word, we must each go to the Book itself for ourselves.

It is as true today as it was when Jesus was on earth that men make the Word of God of none effect through their tradition (Mark 7:13). Yes, the cardinal principle of New Testament Christianity is for each child of God to go straight to the pure fountain of God's Word for himself. Jesus Christ says, *Call no man your father upon the earth: for one is your Father, which is in heaven,* and call no man master, *for one is your Master, even Christ* (Matthew 23:9, 10); that is to say, recognize no absolute spiritual authority, stand in independent relationship to God. In my study of the Book of God, I refuse to bow to the absolute authority of any pope or bishop or priest or any theological professor. I refuse to bow to the Roman Catholic Pope Benedict or to the Protestant Pope Shailer Mathews, or Pope Case, or Pope anybody else. And you on your part should refuse to bow to Pope Torrey or Pope anybody else. Get right to the Book itself, *to the law and to the testimony: if they speak not according to this word, it is because there is no light in them* (Isaiah 8:20). Do not study commentaries, lesson helps, or other books about the Bible; study the Bible itself. Do not study *about* the Bible; study *the Bible.* The Bible is the Word of God, and only the Bible is the Word of God.

A young man who had just graduated from one of our great eastern universities came to Mr. Moody to consult with him as to his lifework. He was a young man belonging to a very wealthy family. Mr. Moody said to him, "Do not go into business. You have more money now than you know what to do with. Why don't you give your life to teaching the English Bible?"

The young man replied, "I don't know anything about the English Bible."

"Why," Mr. Moody exclaimed, "I thought you had just graduated at the university and that they had a high-priced professor employed there for the one purpose of teaching the English Bible."

"Yes," he said, "that is true, and I have taken his classes. But, Mr. Moody, would you like to know how he teaches the English Bible? We have been studying for six months to find out who wrote the Pentateuch, and we know less about it now than when we started." That was not Bible study at all; it was study *about* the Bible. And a good deal of the so-called study of the English Bible today in universities and theological seminaries is of that character.

Every child of God should dig into the Bible itself, entirely independent of all commentaries or all lesson helps. I love to go alone with God and His Book and see what He has to say to me without any man's intervention. The trouble with most of us is that we've been spoon-fed. You go to church Sunday after Sunday, and your pastor ladles out to you what he has found in the Book. Go to the Book itself. I have sometimes watched a robin feed its young and spit into their gaping mouths what it has dug up and chewed. I do not like it. It is doubtless necessary for young robins and chippy birds, but we ought to eventually get beyond that and go right to the Book itself for ourselves.

Study the Bible, Really Study It

Secondly, study the Bible, really study it. That also comes from Acts 17:11: they *searched the scriptures daily, whether those things were so.* Note carefully the word *searched,* or as it is translated in the Revised Standard Version, *examining the scriptures.* The Greek word translated *searched* in the Authorized Version and *examining* in the Revised Standard Version is a very strong word. It means "to search after by looking through, to investigate, to examine, to inquire into, to scrutinize, to sift." It indicates the closest and most minute study. Being God's Book, the Bible is full of meaning in its minutest word and is worthy of not merely the cursory, superficial reading, the careless skimming that most people give to it. That is all most other books, men's books, deserve; any closer study than that is a waste of time. But the Bible, being God's Book, God's own perfect Word, God's inexhaustible storehouse of truth in which are hidden the infinite treasures of the wisdom and knowledge of God, is also worthy of the closest and minutest study.

It abundantly rewards such study, and that is one of the countless proofs that the Bible really is God's Word. The more closely and microscopically you study this Book, the more you see and the more wonderful the blessing you get. The Bible should be studied with the closest and most concentrated attention. Here is where more people miss the fullest blessing in their study of the Bible than anywhere else. They are looking at the Bible with their physical eyes, but their minds are off in a dozen other places. When you study the Bible, resolutely shut everything else out; shut the door of your mind to everything else, and shut yourself up with God alone. It may take time to cultivate this habit of concentrated attention, but any Christian can accomplish it. If you find your mind wandering, go back and fasten your eyes and your mind on that verse again and chew every word. Remember what Jeremiah said: *Thy words were found, and I did eat them; and thy word was unto me the joy and rejoicing of mine heart* (Jeremiah 15:16).

A very prominent and very busy businessman said to me one night, "Tell me in a single word how to study my Bible."

I replied, "It is a pretty big contract to tell a man in a single word how to study the Bible, but if I must put it into one word, this is the word – *thoughtfully*. Study the Bible thoughtfully; give your whole attention to the Bible as you study it."

It is well to read a chapter of the Bible and then close the Book and see how much you can remember. Do the same with single verses. This is one of the greatest secrets of profitable study of any kind – concentrated attention; but it is preeminently the secret of profitable Bible study. The one great objective of the analytical study, verse by verse and word by word, of some books in the Bible that I compel the students in the Bible Institute to do, is to train them in the habit of concentrated attention when they study the Bible. But you do not need to be a student in the Bible Institute to do it; any of you can learn to do it. Not only can every one of you learn to do it, but you also must learn to do it.

Study the Bible Daily

In the third place, study the Bible daily. That also comes from Acts 17:11: *These were more noble than those in Thessalonica, in that they received the word with all readiness of mind, and searched the scriptures daily, whether those things were so.* The daily study of the Bible is the only proper or fully profitable way to study the Bible. We saw in our introduction that proper Bible study was the study that was appropriate or fitting to the Book we were studying, the kind of study of which that Book was worthy. Since the Bible is God's Book, the only kind of study that is fitting to it is everyday study. Don't you desire to know every day what God has to say that day? If you don't, you are a fool. Every Christian who doesn't study, really study, the Bible every day is a fool. Not only that, but any Christian who neglects the study of the Bible one single day also insults God. And you should put much time every day, no matter how busy you are, into Bible study. Certainly, fifteen minutes a day is too little time to put into listening to what God has to say to you. My students think one hour a day is little-enough time to spend with me, and who am I? Who is God? One of the greatest follies of which the average Christian is guilty is spending so little time each day alone with God.

Mr. Moody used to say, "In our prayers we talk to God; in our Bible study God talks to us, and we had better let God do most of the talking." We certainly ought to spend more time every day listening to what God has to say to us in His Word than we require Him to spend in listening to what we have to say to Him in our prayers. Most of us spend too little time in prayer, and almost every one of us spends far too little time in Bible study. Stop and establish a resolution right now that from this time on you will spend more time every day of your life in listening to God as He speaks in His Word, more time in real Bible study.

Study the Bible to Discover
What It Actually Teaches

In the fourth place, study the Bible to discover what it actually teaches. That also comes from Acts 17:11: *they received the word with all readiness of mind, and searched the scriptures daily, whether those things were so.* It comes out in these words: *whether those things were so.* They *searched the scriptures* to find out what they actually taught, not to find out something to corroborate their own previous opinions, but to find out exactly what God had to say. Don't study the Bible to find out what you can make it mean, but to find out what God evidently intended to teach. One of the most prolific sources of misunderstanding and evil in Bible study is found right here. Men go to the Book not to find out what God has to say and what He really means to teach, but to find something that will corroborate their own view or something that they can somehow twist into agreement with their own preconceived opinions.

Take, for example, what the Bible teaches about the second coming of Christ. A host of books and pamphlets have appeared on this subject in the last few years, but many of these do not exhibit the remotest desire to find out what the Bible really has to say on the subject and accept that as final. They are simply a labored and ingenious attempt to discredit what Christ Jesus and the apostles say, or to distort it and make it mean what any fair-minded man or woman in their inmost heart knows it was never intended to mean.

Take, for example, Shailer Mathews' tract "Will Christ Come Again?" From start to finish, it is simply a subtle attempt to discredit the teaching of Jesus Christ and the apostles on this subject. Or take either of the two most lauded books on the second coming written from the postmillennial viewpoint. While they are not so outrageously and blasphemously irreverent in their allusions to the words of our Lord Jesus and the apostles as Shailer Mathews' pamphlet is, they certainly are not an honest, frank, simpleminded attempt to find out exactly what God has to say on the subject. It would be a glaring outrage to study any man's book in that way; it is an atrocious insult to God to study His Book in that way. Study the Bible with an absolutely single-eyed purpose to discover exactly what God intended to teach.

Meditate on What You Find Taught in the Bible

In the fifth place, meditate long and profoundly on what you find taught in the Bible. This is what we are taught in our third text: *Blessed is the man that walketh not in the counsel of the ungodly, nor standeth in the way of sinners, nor sitteth in the seat of the scornful. But his delight is in the law of the LORD; and in his law doth he meditate day and night. And he shall be like a tree planted by the rivers of water, that bringeth forth his fruit in his season; his leaf also shall not wither; and whatsoever he doeth shall prosper* (Psalm 1:1-3).

Since the eternal and all-wise God is the speaker in the Bible, everything taught in the Bible is worthy of our most profound and most prolonged consideration. We should ponder it; we should weigh it; we should thoroughly chew and digest it; we should meditate upon it as we read it and hear it, and afterwards as we go about our daily work, we should meditate upon it *day and night*. Meditation is one of the most fruitful processes of the human mind. But how fruitful and profitable meditation might be depends entirely upon what we meditate on. There is no profit in meditation that is mere mind-wandering and daydreaming. The most fruitful and profitable of all meditation is meditation upon God's revealed truth, God's revealed Word. It is by meditation upon the truth that truth is made productive, just as eggs hatch by being sat upon. *Blessed,* infinitely blessed, is the man that meditates upon the Word of God day and night.

One of the best ways to conserve golden moments that might otherwise be squandered (for example, as we walk the streets or fields or ride on the trolley car) is to meditate upon the Word you have been studying. Turn God's Word over and over and over again in your mind as you study it. Look at all the facets of each diamond of truth. Let the Word soak in; let it saturate your life, your thoughts, your feelings, and your will. Bible-soaked thoughts are God-like thoughts. Bible-soaked affections are God-like affections. A Bible-soaked will is a God-like will. That is a large part of what is meant in John 15:7: *If ye abide in me, and my words abide in you, ye shall ask what ye will, and it shall be done unto you.* Meditate on the Word of God *day and night.*

Store Up the Bible in Your Memory

In the sixth place, growing out of what we have just said, store up the Bible in your memory. Without such storing in memory, the most profitable meditation is impossible. The great profit of storing the Bible in your memory is set forth in Psalm 119:11: *Thy word have I hid in mine heart, that I might not sin against thee.* That is the proper thing to do with God's Word – hide it in your heart. What is so worthy of being treasured in our minds as the golden words of God? Whoever has God's

Word stored away in his mind has treasure vaults filled with pure gold. Our Lord Jesus, as part of His farewell message to His disciples in the wonderful fourteenth chapter of John, verse 21, says, *He that hath my commandments, and keepeth them, he it is that loveth me: and he that loveth me shall be loved of my Father, and I will love him, and will manifest myself to him.*

Don't you long to be one of those whom the Father and the Son love uniquely? Don't you long to have the Lord Jesus *manifest* Himself to you? Well, these words tell you how to secure these priceless privileges: *He that hath my commandments, and keepeth them, he it is that loveth me: and he that loveth me shall be loved of my Father, and I will love him, and will manifest myself to him.* To keep Christ's words means more than simply to obey them; it means to treasure them, to hold on to them, to store them up in your mind and heart, or to use David's phrase – to hide them in your heart.

Then in John 14:23 Jesus says, *If a man love me, he will keep my words: and my Father will love him, and we will come unto him, and make our abode with him.* Isn't that great, having the Father and the Son making their home with us? Well, it is through the treasured-up Word that this is brought about.

Just two suggestions about how to memorize Scripture. First, memorize it systematically. Don't collect a jumble of disjointed texts in your mind, but compile classified and associated texts. Association is the great secret of a retentive memory. Group your memorized passages and classify them in a logical and orderly way. Second, commit the verses to memory by chapter and verse.

Study the Whole Bible

In the seventh place, study the whole Bible. That comes out in a very striking way in Luke 24:27: *And beginning at Moses and all the prophets, he expounded unto them in all the scriptures the things concerning himself.* We see that Jesus studied not merely parts or fragments of the Bible but the whole Bible as far as He had it – *beginning at Moses and all the prophets, he expounded unto them in all the scriptures the things concerning himself.* The whole Bible is the Word of God; therefore, every part of the Bible should be studied. We not only need to know the mind of God, but we also need the whole mind of God.

One of the most common causes of comparatively unprofitable Bible study is that only parts of the Bible are studied. Some only study pet books. Some study only the New Testament; some study only the Psalms; some never study Genesis; some never study prophecy; they never study Revelation, and they never study Daniel. Others study nothing but Daniel or Revelation. Some study only pet subjects. Some never study anything but divine healing, and some never study divine healing at all. Some never study the second coming of Christ, and others never study anything but the second coming of Christ. You never rightly understand any one of the sixty-six books of the Bible until you study it in its relation to the other sixty-five. You never rightly understand any subject in the Bible until you understand it in its relationship to other subjects in the Bible.

Study the Bible As the Word of God

In the eighth place, study the Bible as the Word of God. We are taught to do this by God Himself in 1 Thessalonians 2:13: *For this cause also thank we God without ceasing, because, when ye received the word of God which ye heard of us, ye received it not as the word of men, but as it is in truth, the word of God, which effectually worketh also in you that believe.*

We have already seen that the proper way to study any book is to study it just as it is. Then it is as clear as day that since the Bible is the Word of God, the proper way to study it and the only proper way to study it, the only way to get the largest profit out of the study of it, is to study it as the Word of God.

Many distinguished university professors say we should study the Bible just as we study any other book, and they imagine that they have said something wondrously wise when they have said it. But while it is partly true, it is very largely false; indeed, it is very largely shameless nonsense. We should study the Bible as we study any other book to this extent: we should apply the same laws for the discovery of the meaning of words and phrases and the same laws of grammatical construction to it that we apply to any other book, but there the principle ceases. We should study it as we study no other book, for it is what no other book is: it is God's Word, and all other books are men's words. We should study it as what it is, and we should study other books as what they are. So we should study the Bible, and the Bible alone, as God's Word, and we should study all other books as men's words, for that is exactly what they are.

What is involved in studying the Bible as God's Word? Five things:

First, we must believe absolutely every statement. We may not see how it can be true, but we should believe it simply because God says it. Abraham could not see how he, when he was about a hundred years old and Sarah nearly as old and childless, could become *a father of many nations,* but God said so and Abraham believed it, and God *counted it to him for righteousness* (Genesis 15:6). If we have good sense, we will behave just like Abraham. God says something in this Book; Professor So-and-so says it is not so. The Reverend Dr. Bighead, D.D., Ph.D., L.L.D., Litt.D., F.R.G.S. says it cannot be so; but since God says so, you and I, if we have real good sense, will believe it in spite of all the so-and-sos in the world.

In the second place, we must trust its every promise in all its height and depth and length and breadth unhesitatingly and without a trace of doubt or anxiety lest it fail us. I am only a frail and feeble man, but I expect every man to accept and rest absolutely upon every promise of mine. And God, who cannot lie (Titus 1:2), not only expects that of you and me, but He also demands it, and you are a fool if you do not do it. Many of the promises of this Book seem altogether too big to believe, but God made them, and there is nothing too big for God. Not a promise in this Book ever failed yet, if you put both your feet upon it. I have found that out by thirty-six years of experience. This Book tells me that I am an heir of God and a joint-heir with Jesus Christ; it promises me that I am to inherit all God is and all God has. It looks ridiculous to me, but I believe it. God says it, and therefore I believe it. I would be a fool if I did not.

In the third place, studying the Bible as the Word of God involves obeying implicitly and exactly its every commandment that is addressed to you. There are commandments in this Book that are not addressed to you; the Bible explicitly says that they are addressed to Jews, and you are not a Jew. But many commandments are addressed to you; obey every one of them to the last jot and tittle. It will seem hard sometimes, but it will pay.

In the fourth place, studying the Bible as the Word of God involves studying it as God's message to you, not as God's Word in the abstract but God's Word in the concrete – God's Word to you. Forget everybody else for the time being, and think of God as saying this thing to you. Oh, it is fine to have a talk with God and to have Him do the talking. He has so much more to say that is worth listening to than you or I have to say to Him. I know a man in China who has the rare gift of keeping his mouth shut in seven different languages. He is quite a young man, but he has acquired a great reputation for wisdom because he so seldom says anything.

He listens. But the place of places to keep still is when you are studying the Bible; keep still and listen and let God do the talking.

In the fifth place, studying the Bible as the Word of God involves studying the Book as in the presence of God. See God standing right there saying these things that are written. Have you never thought, when you have read how God came down and talked with Abraham face to face, that you wished He could come down and talk that way with you? Well, we have a privilege far beyond that of Abraham. It was only in a few rare instances that God came down and met Abraham and talked with him, but God is ready to come down and meet us and talk with us face to face every time we open our Bibles. Oh, it is great to have God call you into His presence and say, "I have something I want to whisper right into your ear alone and into your heart," and then open your Bible and see God standing there and hear Him saying that which is written there in the Book in front of your eyes. Studying the Bible that way makes the Bible a new and living Book. It is great to study the Bible on your knees. It has been one of the rarest privileges of my life to read every chapter in the Bible and every verse in the Bible on my knees. And it is your privilege to do the same.

Study the Bible with a Will
Wholly Surrendered to God

In the ninth place, study the Bible with a will wholly surrendered to God. That is one of the greatest secrets of proper and profitable Bible study. Nothing clears up the mind to see and understand what God says and what God means like a will wholly surrendered to Him. Our Lord Jesus Himself teaches that. He says, *If any man will do his will, he shall know of the doctrine, whether it be of God, or whether I speak of myself* (John 7:17). The mind of the man whose will is not surrendered to God is a fogbank; the mind of the man whose will is surrendered to God is clear shining as a perfect California day. Oh, I have known men to whom the Bible was a sealed book, a useless book, a silly, stupid book, but by the unreserved surrender of their wills to God, the Bible became an open book. The surrender of the will to God will do more to make the Bible an open book than a university education at home and abroad in Greek and Hebrew and similar languages.

I have known great Greek scholars and great Hebrew scholars who were as blind as a bat to the real meaning of God's Word simply because their wills were not surrendered to God. I have known men and women who knew none of the original languages in which the Bible was written, neither the original Greek nor the original Hebrew, but only knew the original English, who were open-eyed to all that was best and dearest in this Book because their wills were utterly surrendered to God.

We had a young woman in the Bible Institute in Chicago years ago who seemed to have no fitness to be a student at a Bible institute. She was entirely out of harmony with the place, and densely ignorant of the things of God. One day she went (as all the women students were required to go now and then) down to one of the destitute parts of the city, calling from house to house upon the poor. She became utterly disgusted with the surroundings and quit her work; she went down to Lake Shore Drive and walked along in front of the magnificent mansions. She said to herself, "Now, this is what I like, and this is what I am going to have. I am thoroughly sick of Milton Avenue and Townsend Street. This is for me." In that rebellious state of mind, she returned to the Institute, and the bell soon rang for supper. She went down and took her seat at the table, still rebelling at the thought of a life of sacrifice amid unpleasant surroundings. But suddenly, there at the supper table, she surrendered her will to God, sprang from the table, rushed over to one of the other girls, and threw her arms around her. She said, "I am a volunteer for Africa." A wonderful transformation and a wonderful opening of her mind to the things of God occurred instantly.

I was away when this happened, but when I came back, my secretary told me about it, for it was the talk of the school. A little later in the day as I passed out of the gate on La Salle Avenue, I met this young woman coming in. She looked up radiantly into my face and said, "Oh, Mr. Torrey, have you heard the news?"

I said, "Yes, Miss Waite has told me."

Then she fairly danced in glee on the sidewalk as she poured out her glad heart, and then she said, "Oh, Mr. Torrey, the most wonderful thing about it is that the Bible is a new book. I thought the Bible was the most stupid book in the world. I would rather have read an old almanac than the Bible. You compelled me by your lectures at Northfield to believe in the deity of Christ, but the Bible I could not endure. But oh, since I surrendered my will, what a wonderful book the Bible is; God is making marvelous revelations to me from it every day."

Oh, men and women, if you want a Bible that is wonderful, a Bible where every page glows with glory, study it with a will absolutely surrendered to God.

Study the Bible to Learn How to Live Your Daily Life

In the tenth place, study the Bible to learn how to live your daily life, and live your daily life that way. God commands us to do this in James 1:22. He says, *Be ye doers of the word, and not hearers only, deceiving your own selves.* Many study the Bible; yes, they dig into it and spend hours with it just to gratify their curiosity on the great biblical subjects or to qualify themselves as expert theological debaters. No, no, no! Study the Bible to discover how to live so as to please God and then live that way. Studying the Bible with an eager desire to learn how to please God and living that way goes a long way toward making the Bible an open book. People often ask what is the best translation of the original Scriptures, the Authorized Version or the Revised Version or Weymouth's or another translation. Listen, infinitely the best translation of the Bible is the translation into daily living.

Study the Bible under the Holy Spirit's Personal Direction

In the eleventh place, study the Bible under the Holy Spirit's personal direction. God tells us, *But the natural man receiveth not the things of the Spirit of God: for they are foolishness unto him: neither can he know them, because they are spiritually discerned* (1 Corinthians 2:14). Don't study the Bible as the Christian Scientist studies it – through Mrs. Eddy's spectacles under bondage to science and health. Mrs. Eddy's spectacles are badly smoked glasses. Don't study the Bible as Pastor Russell's dupes study it – through that silly man's spectacles, trying to see the Bible with "millennial dawn" standing between you and the Book of God itself. Don't study it as the Mormon studies it – looking at the Bible through the densely opaque medium of the ridiculous and immoral Book of Mormon.

Call no man your father [master] (Matthew 23:9). Don't study the Bible through any man's spectacles; study it through the telescope and microscope of the Holy Spirit. Study it under the personal direction of the Holy Spirit. The way to obtain His personal direction in your study of the Bible is expressed in Psalm 119:18: *Open thou mine eyes, that I may behold wondrous things out of thy law.* It is by asking for it. *If ye then, being evil, know how to give good gifts unto your children: how much more shall your heavenly Father give the Holy Spirit to them that ask him?* (Luke 11:13). We are also told in Luke 24:45: *Then opened he their understanding, that they might understand the scriptures.*

Study the Bible with a Childlike Mind

Finally, study the Bible with a childlike mind. That is the only proper way to study the Bible, for the Bible is a revelation intended by God to be understood by all honest-minded, humble-minded, teachable people. Many scholarly men study the Bible as if it were a puzzle book; instead of taking the meaning that lies on the surface, they dig down for some occult meaning, some meaning other than what the words seem to imply.

The Roman Catholic Church says that simpleminded Christians must not dare to study the Bible for themselves independently; they must go to the priest to interpret it for them. The University of Chicago says that ordinary, unscholarly, regenerate men, women, and children cannot get the Bible's real meaning for themselves; they must have some great scholar, soaked in the German infidelity of Wellhausen and Graf and their host of satellites and followers, to interpret it for them.

But Jesus said, *I thank thee, O Father, Lord of heaven and earth, because thou hast hid these things from the wise and prudent, and hast revealed them unto babes* (Matthew 11:25). Oh, these ingenious and fantastic interpretations of cunning scholars, men who are so subtle that they are positively silly! They would be laughable if they were not outrageous. Some men's intellect

47

is very close to perdition. The little girl was right when she said, "If God didn't mean what He said, why didn't He say what He meant?" He does say what He means, exactly what He means.

Study the Bible Systematically

Once more, study the Bible systematically. It is very clear from Luke 24:27 that Jesus so studied it, for we read, *And beginning at Moses and all the prophets, he expounded unto them in all the scriptures the things concerning himself.* Use some good system of Bible study and follow it. System counts in everything, but it counts more in study than it counts in anything else, and it counts more in Bible study than in any other form of study, though I don't have time here to go into the details of systems or methods of Bible study.

Let me add just one word: improve spare moments for Bible study. Carry a Bible with you wherever you go, or at least a New Testament, and whenever you have a spare moment, put it into Bible study. But don't be content only with the use of spare moments in Bible study; have a regular set time every day that is kept sacredly for getting alone with God in the study of His Word.

Chapter 3

How to Interpret the Bible to Find Its True Meaning

For we are not as many, which corrupt the word of God: but as of sincerity, but as of God, in the sight of God speak we in Christ. (2 Corinthians 2:17)

Therefore seeing we have this ministry, as we have received mercy, we faint not; but have renounced the hidden things of dishonesty, not walking in craftiness, nor handling the word of God deceitfully; but by manifestation of the truth commending ourselves to every man's conscience in the sight of God. But if our gospel be hid, it is hid to them that are lost: in whom the god of this world hath blinded the minds of them which believe not, lest the light of the glorious gospel of Christ, who is the image of God, should shine unto them. (2 Corinthians 4:1-4)

Study to shew thyself approved unto God, a workman that needeth not to be ashamed, rightly dividing the word of truth. (2 Timothy 2:15)

The devil . . . saith unto him, . . . it is written. (Matthew 4:5-6)

My next subject is how to interpret the Bible to find its true meaning. I have four texts. The first is that *we are not as many, which corrupt the word of God: but as of sincerity, but as of God, in the sight of God speak we in Christ* (2 Corinthians 2:17). The word translated *corrupt* in this verse is derived from a noun meaning "a tavern keeper, a wine merchant, a petty retailer, a huckster, or a peddler." The thought is that as tavern keepers and wine merchants and peddlers frequently adulterate their wines, fruits, or other wares, so many alleged teachers of the Word of God adulterate the Word of God. That is certainly true of not a few preachers, Bible teachers, and theological professors in America and elsewhere in these days. Paul says he was not in that contemptible, disreputable business, and we ought to be careful that we are not either, when we teach or when we study God's Word.

Our second text is 2 Corinthians 4:1-4:

> *Therefore seeing we have this ministry,*
> *as we have received mercy, we faint not;*
> *but have renounced the hidden things of*
> *dishonesty, not walking in craftiness, nor*
> *handling the word of God deceitfully; but*
> *by manifestation of the truth commending*
> *ourselves to every man's conscience in the*
> *sight of God. But if our gospel be hid, it is*
> *hid to them that are lost [are perishing]: in*
> *whom the god of this world hath blinded the*
> *minds of them which believe not, lest the*
> *light of the glorious gospel of Christ, who is*
> *the image of God, should shine unto them.*

The word translated *handling deceitfully* in these verses means "to corrupt," as metals are debased or wine adulterated, and the thought is that of debasing the pure gold of God's Word, or adulterating the pure wine of God's Word, by mingling false ideas with it. That too is a common practice today. Paul says that he has *renounced the hidden things of dishonesty,* and that he is *not walking in [theological] craftiness [cunning or subtlety].* It is evident that he did not have the "advantage" of an education in some of our American institutions, as he was not debasing the pure gold of the Word of God or adulterating the pure wine of the Word of God by mixing in his own preconceived notions. Here too we also greatly need to be on our guard when we study or teach the Word of God.

Our third text is, *Study to shew thyself approved unto God, a workman that needeth not to be ashamed, rightly dividing the word of truth* (2 Timothy 2:15). The Authorized Version, as you know, reads, *Study to shew thyself approved unto God, a workman that needeth not to be ashamed, rightly dividing the word of truth.* The Greek word for *rightly dividing* that Paul actually used means "cutting straight," and that would be a better way to translate it here than the way it is rendered in either the Authorized Version or the Revised Version. Then the verse would read: *Give diligence to present thyself approved unto God, a workman that needeth not to be ashamed, [cutting straight] the word of truth* (RV). I tell you there is a lot of crooked cutting today when men come to the study and interpretation of the Word of God, especially when they find something they do not wish to believe.

Some years ago, a friend of mine passed by a carpenter

52

and joiner's shop in a southern city. Over the door was this sign: "All sorts of twisting and turning done here." That would be a fine sign to put over the door of some of our theological seminaries, many of our pulpits and Bible classes, and many a room where Christians are studying the Word of God alone. Each one of us needs to be on our guard that this may not be an appropriate sign over the door of the room where we study our Bible alone. Remember as you study the Bible that it is God's Word, and be sure to "cut it straight."

My fourth text is Matthew 4:5-6: *The devil . . . saith unto him, . . . it is written.* You see from this passage that the devil can quote Scripture and interpret or misinterpret Scripture and argue from what *is written* in the Book of God. If you think he has quit the business, read Pastor Russell's *Millennial Dawn* or Mrs. Eddy's *Science and Health* or some of the productions of the American Institute of Sacred Literature or the University of Chicago or some of the Sunday school helps sent out by some of our denominational boards. But I would not advise you to spend much time on this devil-inspired trash.

It is not enough to study the Bible or even to spend several hours in Bible study daily. We must seek diligently to cut it straight. We must find out how to interpret the Bible to find its true meaning, to discover just what God meant to teach by each verse we study, and then interpret it that way in every instance. Of many passages of Scripture there are several possible meanings; one man says it means one thing, and another man says it means another thing. Now God intends only one of these meanings. We should seek to find out not what men say it means, even good men, but what God intended it to teach. Is there any way in which ordinary men like you and me can tell with certainty which interpretation of several possible interpretations of a passage is the right interpretation, the exact meaning God intended to convey? There is. There are certain "laws of interpretation" that will enable you to know in almost every instance just what is the true interpretation of every verse in the Bible, what is the true sense of the passage – just what God wishes to teach. I shall endeavor to state these laws so you can all understand them and then apply them for yourselves.

Get Right with God by the Surrender of Your Will to God

The first great law of correct Bible interpretation, which will be recognized as a law of God by any fair-minded person who gives it a few minutes' consideration, is to get absolutely right with God by the absolute surrender of your will to Him. The only man who is at all competent to interpret the will of God is the man who is in harmony with God, and the only man who is in harmony with God is the man whose will is fully surrendered to God. If you are not right with God, you certainly are not competent to say what God means by any passage in His Word. Our Lord Jesus Himself says, *If any man will do his will, he shall know of the doctrine, whether it be of God, or whether I speak of myself* (John 7:17). Nothing else so clears up our minds to understand the Word of God as the surrender of our will to God.

The will is the eye of the soul. Our Lord also says that. He says, *The light of the body is the eye: if therefore thine eye be single, thy whole body shall be full of light. But if thine eye be evil, thy whole body shall be full of darkness* (Matthew 6:22-23). And it is clear from the next verse that by a *single eye* He means a will fully surrendered to God. His words are, *No man can serve two masters: for either he will hate the one, and love the other; or else he will hold to the one, and despise the other* (Matthew 6:24). If your will is surrendered to God and to Him alone, your *eye [is] single*, and your *whole body [is] full of light*. But if your will is not fully surrendered to God and Him alone, your *eye [is] evil*, and your whole person is *full of darkness*. Nothing gives us as clear an eye to discern as we read God's Word, just what God means, as an entirely surrendered will.

A surrendered will does more to qualify anyone to be a competent and dependable interpreter of the Word of God than the fullest possible university course in Greek and Hebrew and the related languages. As I said before, I have known great Greek scholars and great Hebrew scholars and men deeply versed in the related languages who were as blind as a bat to the real meaning of the Scriptures because they lacked that clearness of spiritual vision that comes only from a surrendered will. And on the other hand, I have known very ordinary and quite uneducated men and women with no pretensions whatever to scholarship who had a wonderful understanding of the meaning of God's Word because their wills were surrendered to God.

We get this same principle of Bible interpretation from Psalm 25:14: *The secret [the friendship] of the LORD is with them that fear him; and he will shew them his covenant.* The same thought is found in Proverbs 3:32: *For the froward is abomination to the LORD: but his secret is with the righteous.* A closely similar thought is found in our Lord's last words to His disciples on the night before His crucifixion: *Henceforth I call you not servants; for the servant knoweth not what his lord doeth: but I have called you friends; for all things that I have heard of my Father I have made known unto you* (John 15:15).

The first great principle of biblical interpretation, then, is that the one who would interpret the Bible must himself be in harmony with the Author of the Book by the surrender of his will to God. Every theological professor whose will is not fully surrendered to God should be turned out of the chair he occupies in any seminary or university.

When Mr. Alexander and I were holding meetings in a university city in England, Mr. Alexander was invited out to dinner by one of the most prominent officers in one of the theological schools connected to the university. This man, who was a fine man in many ways, took exception to some of our teachings. He accompanied Mr. Alexander after dinner out to his carriage, and as they stood by the carriage and had a few earnest parting words, Mr. Alexander put the question straight to him: "Have you ever made a full surrender of your will to God?"

This prominent theological university teacher very frankly and gently said to Mr. Alexander, "No, Mr. Alexander, I have not." That accounted for his misunderstanding of the Word of God, and the same thing accounts for the misunderstanding of the Word of God on the part of a great many students of the Word today.

See to it that you are not blinded in a similar way to the real meaning of God's Word. Unless you fulfill this first great law of correct Bible interpretation, it will not help you to fulfill the other laws. You will get nowhere in your study of the Word.

Be Determined to Discover What God Intended to Teach

The second principle of correct Bible interpretation is to be determined to discover what God intended to teach and not what you wish Him to teach. One great reason why many do not find the true meaning of God's words is that they do not really wish to find the true meaning of God's words, but they wish to find some way in which they can force God's words into harmony with their own notions. Many men and women see only what they wish to see in the Bible. This is the cause of the blinding of the eyes of many.

Someone asked me the other day, "Why can't the Jews see that their own Old Testament Scriptures predicted a suffering Messiah who would make atonement for sin by His death, and that Jesus is that Messiah? It is so plain."

The answer is simple – because they are spiritually blinded.[3]

And then I asked that person a question. "Why don't Christians today see that there are other predictions in the Old Testament just as plain and far more of them that the Messiah is coming as an all-conquering King to rule the nations with a rod of iron, and that Jesus, the true Messiah, is coming again?" The answer to that is just as simple – cares of the world and temptations are choking out what really matters.[4]

Many years ago I was certain that all men would ultimately be saved and the devil too. I was so determined to establish that doctrine that I interpreted everything I found in the Bible on the subject of future punishment in the light, or rather in the darkness, of that determination of mine in order to make the Bible square with my own view, which I reasoned philosophically and was ready to defend against all newcomers. But when I reached the point where I desired not only to make the Bible square with my philosophical arguments for universal salvation but also to find out just what God really taught, I easily found what God did teach. My universal-salvation arguments evaporated into thin air. We must all be on our guard at this point;

---

3   Romans 11:25
4   Mark 4:18-20

in absolute honesty we must have only one wish – to discover what God means by the verse we are studying and only that, no matter how much it may conflict with our previous ideas.

Get the Most Accurate Text

The third principle of correct Bible interpretation is to get the most accurate text to interpret. The original manuscripts of the Bible are the very Word of God. Now, we do not have the original manuscripts of the Bible. We have many manuscripts, but not one of them is the original. There are many variations in the manuscripts which we possess. But by a comparison of the many manuscripts of the various parts of the Bible, and we have far more manuscripts of the books of the Bible than of any other ancient book, we can come close to the original texts as they came from the hands of Paul, John, Matthew, and the rest of the writers of the books of the Old and New Testaments. Indeed, we now have what is to all practical intents and purposes the original text as it came from the hand of the original writers of the various books of the Bible.

It is wonderful when we remember how old these books are, how often they were copied, how many manuscripts we have, and the advances in scholarship, especially in textual criticism, that have been made in the time between when the Authorized Version was published in 1611, and when the Revised Version was published only a few years ago in 1881, yet there are few differences of real importance between the Authorized Version and the Revised Version. There is not one single doctrine of any vital importance affected in the least by the variations between the two versions – not one. That is amazing, and it shows the wonderful providential care with which God guarded His own written Word. But there are slight differences, and of course, we wish to know the exact mind of God; and since that is found in the original manuscripts, we therefore desire and should seek the purest text, the most exact text, the text that is closest to the original manuscripts. There can be no honest question that the Revised Version presents a text more exactly the same as that of the original manuscripts than the Authorized Version does. So, though for many reasons the Authorized Version is the better one for the general reading of the average Christian, nevertheless, everyone who wishes to find the exact words of God should have and should study the Revised Version.

There is one glaring misrendering in the Revised Version, however. It is found in 2 Timothy 3:16. The Revised Version reads, *Every scripture inspired of God is also profitable for teaching, for reproof, for correction, for instruction which is in righteousness,* putting the *is* after the *inspired of God* instead of before it as in the Authorized Version. There is absolutely no reason for this change. It is indefensible. It should read, "Every scripture is inspired of God and is profitable for teaching, for reproof, for correction, for instruction in righteousness." But the fault in that case is not in the Greek text upon which the Revised Version is built, but upon the translation of the text. There is no question about the Greek text even in this case. Many uncertainties about the meaning of various passages in the Bible would be easily settled if we would just look at the more correct text as given in the Revised Version.

Take 1 Thessalonians 5:22 as an illustration. The Authorized Version renders this, *Abstain from all appearance of evil;* the Revised Version renders it, *Abstain from every form of evil.* While the Greek text that King James translators and the revisers used is the same, I think the English text in the Revised Version gives the true sense of the Greek text better than the Authorized Version does. We are not so much to *abstain from [the] appearance of evil,* but from what is actually evil, and from what is actually evil in every form in which it appears, *every form of evil.*

Find the Most Exact and Literal
Meaning of the Text

The fourth principle of correct Bible interpretation is to find the most exact and literal meaning of the text. It is one of the most firmly established principles of law in England and in America that "a law stands as it is written"; in other words, a law means exactly what it says and is to be interpreted and enforced just as it reads. This is as good a principle for interpreting the Bible as for interpreting law. If Shailer Mathews and the rest of the higher critics and "new theology" men were practicing law and tried to interpret laws in any court of justice as they interpret the Bible, they would be laughed out of court. It is no wonder that the one who has done more to prick the iridescent soap bubbles of the higher critics and new-theology men than almost anyone else was a brilliant lawyer, knighted by King Edward for his eminent legal talents – my late intimate and beloved friend Sir Robert Anderson. The primary meaning of any passage of Scripture, just as the meaning of any law on our statute books, is the literal meaning, unless it is perfectly plain from the context, from other Scripture, or from the manifestly figurative character of the passage that something else than the literal sense is intended.

Those who do not wish in any particular case to accept what God actually says, including some who are scholars who ought to know better, often flee from the plain meaning of a text. They say, "Oh, but you know that *the letter killeth, but the spirit giveth life,*" by which they mean the *literal sense* of a passage, the interpretation that takes God as meaning just what He says – *killeth,* but a *spiritual interpretation,* an interpretation that makes God mean something He does not say – *giveth life.* If anyone will look up Paul's words, *the letter killeth, but the spirit giveth life* (2 Corinthians 3:6) in their context, he will see that Paul never dreamed of such an interpretation or application of his words as these men give to them. It is as clear as day from the context that what Paul meant was that the mere written letter, written with ink or engraved *in tables of stone,* killed, but the Word of God, written *with the Spirit of the living God* on our hearts, *in tables that are hearts of flesh,* gives life (2 Corinthians 3:3 RV). These men who thus misuse 2 Corinthians 3:6 call those who hold fast to the actual literal meaning of the words "deadly literalists." But if that kind of literalism is deadly, then Paul himself, the very one who wrote these words, was one of the most deadly literalists the world has ever known, for Paul constantly insisted upon the literal meaning of words and would build an argument upon the tense, number, or case of a word used.

A very distinguished Hebrew scholar, a professor in a leading American theological seminary, once tried to work this interpretation of 2 Corinthians 3:6 on me. In a friendly discussion, I had driven him into a corner by quoting a plain statement from God's Word. He could not escape, but tried to sidestep by saying, "But you know that *the letter killeth, but the spirit giveth life.*"

I replied, "Now Professor, do you really think that is what Paul means by those words?"

And he frankly said, "No, I know it is not."

Another very easy and common way of reading out of the Bible what God has put into it is for men to say, "Oh, that is figurative," when they are driven into a corner by some plain passage that they do not wish to believe. By this they mean it does not mean what it says, but you can take it to mean whatever you like. That is a common tactic today with the postmillennialists – reading out of the Bible what God so plainly says in it about the personal, visible, bodily, imminent coming again of our Lord Jesus. It is outrageous trickery, unworthy of anyone who has sense enough to subordinate his own crude and fallible opinions to the plain teaching and infinite wisdom of God's Word. When statements are plainly figurative, of course, interpret them as figures, but even then remember that figures stand for facts, and God's figures never overstate the facts and never misinterpret the facts; an honest man's figures never mean just the opposite of what they seem to teach.

The most plain and obvious meaning of any passage in the Bible is always to be preferred to a subtle and ingenious one, for the Bible was written for plain, honest-minded, humble-minded, common folk, and not for a few refined mystics. Didn't Jesus say, *I thank thee, O Father, Lord of heaven and earth, because thou hast hid these things from the wise and prudent, and hast revealed them unto babes. Even so, Father: for so it seemed good in thy sight* (Matthew 11:25-26)? Well, don't forget it.

A man who was a great scholar once said at a Bible conference, "I think the best method of Bible study is the baby method," by which he meant just what Jesus Christ means here – that God reveals His truth to the humble, teachable mind, to the one who comes to Him as a babe. Remember how Jesus said again, *Except ye be converted, and become as little children, ye shall not enter into the kingdom of heaven* (Matthew 18:3).

Note the Exact Force of Each Word Used

The fifth principle of correct Bible interpretation is

to note the exact force of each word used. Remember that the Bible is God's Word and that God always says exactly what He means – no more, no less. Remember that the Bible is verbally inspired; the Holy Spirit, the unerring Spirit of God, led the Bible writers in the choice of every word they wrote. He led them to write the word that exactly expressed what was in the mind of God, or as Paul puts it, *Which things also we speak, not in the words which man's wisdom teacheth, but which the Holy Spirit teacheth; comparing spiritual things with spiritual* (1 Corinthians 2:13). Note every word and the exact force of every word.

Take, for example, Revelation 2:10: *Be thou faithful unto death, and I will give thee a crown of life.* Now this is constantly interpreted as meaning that we are saved by being faithful unto death, but it does not say so. It says, *Be thou faithful unto death, and I will give thee a crown of life.* It tells us not the way to be saved, but the way to obtain the crown.

Take Luke 6:30: *Give to every man that asketh of thee.* This is constantly interpreted as if it meant "Give to every man that asketh thee, *just what he asks,*" but it does not say that; it says, *Give to every man that asketh,* but does not specify what to give to him. And it means exactly and literally what it says. It is far better to give some men advice than it is to give them money.

The whole context shows we are to take God as our example in our giving and in all else that we do, and while God gives to everyone who asks, He certainly does not always give, even to His own children, the very thing we have asked.

Take Ephesians 4:30: *Grieve not the holy Spirit of God, whereby ye are sealed unto the day of redemption.* This is constantly interpreted as meaning that we are not to "grieve away the Holy Spirit." But it does not say that. So far from teaching us that we can grieve away the Holy Spirit, it tells us in the last part of the verse that we cannot: *Whereby ye are sealed unto the day of redemption.* But while we cannot grieve Him away, if we are children of God, we can grieve Him, and alas, we do.

Interpret the Words Used
According to Bible Usage

The sixth great principle of correct Bible interpretation is to interpret the words used in any verse according to the Bible usage of those words. When some people find any new word in the Bible, they run off for *Webster's Dictionary* or the *Standard Dictionary* to find out just what the word means. No, go to the Bible. Take your concordance and look up every passage in which the word in question is used, and you will have God's definition of its meaning.

For example, take the word *death*. In Romans 6:23 we read, *For the wages of sin is death; but the gift of God is eternal life through Jesus Christ our Lord.* What does *death* mean here? Many run off to a dictionary and decide it means "cessation of existence"; but take your Bible and concordance and go through the Bible, and you will find it means nothing of the kind in the Bible. God Himself defines the *death,* which is the ultimate result of sin in Revelation 21:8: *But the fearful, and unbelieving, and the abominable, and murderers, and whoremongers, and sorcerers, and idolators, and all liars, shall have their part in the lake which burneth with fire and brimstone: which is the second death.*

A man came into my office in Minneapolis. This text was hanging among others upon the wall, and he read, "*The wages of sin is death,*" and then he turned to me and said, "Do you believe that?"

I knew the man was an annihilationist, and I said, "Yes sir, I believe it, but do you know what *death* means?" I took my Bible and showed him that his understanding of the word *death* was not the Bible meaning, and I think I convinced him of his error.

Take the word *sanctify,* a word of frequent occurrence in the Bible. Many define the word for themselves and take it to mean "to make absolutely holy in character." They build a whole system of theology, and an utterly false system of theology, on their wrong definition. If they would take their Bibles and concordances and look up every one of the many passages in the Bible where this word is used, they would find that the primary meaning of *to sanctify* is "to set apart for God." They would find that the Bible-teaching on this exceedingly precious and important subject of sanctification is entirely different from what they suppose. Likewise with the word *justify* and a multitude of other words. When you are in doubt as to the exact meaning of any word in the Bible, take your concordance and look up every verse in the Bible where the word is used, and you will see what the word means.

Interpret the Words with Regard to the Particular Usage of That Author

The seventh principle of correct Bible interpretation is closely connected with the sixth. It is to interpret the words of each author in the Bible with regard to the particular usage of that author. While God is the real Author of every book in the Bible, He used the individual personality of each man He employed to write the various books which make up His own Word. So we should find how the particular writer that we are studying uses any word.

For example, James does not use the words *faith* and *believe* in the exact sense that Paul uses them or in the exact sense in which John uses them. When James talks about "believing," he means a mere intellectual conviction of the truth, so he says, *The devils also believe, and tremble* (James 2:19).

Paul speaks of "believing" as a conviction that governs a man's whole inner life: his intellect, his emotions, and his will. He says, *If thou shalt confess with thy mouth the Lord Jesus, and shalt believe in thine heart that God hath raised him from the dead, thou shalt be saved. For with the heart man believeth unto righteousness; and with the mouth confession is made unto salvation* (Romans 10:9-10).

And he said to the Philippian jailer, *Believe on the Lord Jesus Christ, and thou shalt be saved* (Acts 16:31).

Also, when John speaks of "believing," he means a conviction to which a man utterly, unreservedly, and gladly surrenders himself. So he says in John 20:31, *These are written, that ye might believe that Jesus is the Christ, the Son of God; and that believing ye might have life through his name.* And he says in 1 John 5:1, *Whosoever believeth that Jesus is the Christ is born of God;* and four verses later he says, *Who is he that overcometh the world, but he that believeth that Jesus is the Son of God?*

Interpret Individual Verses with Regard to the Context

The eighth principle of correct Bible interpretation is to interpret individual verses with regard to the context. Many a verse might mean two or three or more different things if it stood alone without any setting, but in its context in the Bible, taking note of what goes before it and what comes after it, it cannot mean but one of these three or four different things. So we must notice carefully what comes before the verse we are studying and what comes after it, if we are to discover the exact meaning of the verse before us.

For example, take Acts 2:39: *For the promise is unto you, and to your children, and to all that are afar off, even as many as the Lord our God shall call.* Now what is *the promise* to which reference is made in this passage? Some say it is the promise of salvation; others say it is the promise to the individual of the baptism with the Holy Spirit. Which one is right? If the verse stood alone, either one might be right. But when we look at it in its context, only one meaning is seen to be the true sense. Read the verse that goes immediately before it:

Then Peter said unto them, Repent, and be baptized every one of you in the name of Jesus Christ for the remission of sins, and ye shall receive the gift of the Holy Spirit (Acts 2:38). Then he goes on immediately to say, *For the promise is unto you* – what promise? The promise, of course, of which he has just spoken, *the promise of the gift of the Holy Spirit.*

Take John 14:18: *I will not leave you comfortless: I will come to you.* To what "coming" does this refer? To the second coming of Christ or to His coming in the Holy Spirit to dwell in their hearts? It might mean either, if it stood alone. But if you read the two verses that immediately precede it, and the five verses immediately following it, you will see it refers to His coming in the Holy Spirit to dwell in their hearts. In the verses that immediately precede it, He says, *And I will pray the Father, and he shall give you another Comforter, that he may abide with you for ever; even the Spirit of truth; whom the world cannot receive, because it seeth him not, neither knoweth him: but ye know him; for he dwelleth with you, and shall be in you* (John 14:16-17).

This becomes clearer in the verses that follow, where He speaks of the coming of the Holy Spirit in which He will manifest Himself to them and will come and make His abode with them.

Interpret Individual Passages in the Light of Parallel or Related Passages

The ninth principle of correct biblical interpretation is to interpret individual passages in the light of parallel or related passages. The meaning of many passages in the Gospels whose meaning seems doubtful would be settled at once if one would only read the parallel passages in another Gospel.

Take, for example, Luke 14:26-27: *If any man come to me, and hate not his father, and mother, and wife, and children, and brethren, and sisters, yea, and his own life also, he cannot be my disciple. And whosoever doth not bear his cross, and come after me, cannot be my disciple.*

Now that looks hard. It has puzzled more people than almost any other passage in the Bible. But turn to the parallel passage in Matthew 10:37-38, and it is cleared up. *He that loveth father or mother more than me is not worthy of me: and he that loveth son or daughter more than me is not worthy of me. And he that taketh not his cross, and followeth after me, is not worthy of me.*

So it is evident that our Lord Jesus used the word *hate* in Luke 14:26-27 in a sense in which it is used a number of times in the Bible – as a comparatively less love. Our love for God should be so immeasurably superior to our love for even the dearest of our earthly relatives, that in comparison with our love for God, our attitude toward them would be like aversion or turning away from them.

Take John 14:3: *I will come again, and receive you unto myself; that where I am, there ye may be also.* Now our Lord might be referring to His coming again to receive us at death, or He might be referring to His second coming. To which does He refer? Another passage clearly and unmistakably answers the question. First Thessalonians 4:16-17 says, *For the Lord himself shall descend from heaven with a shout, with the voice of the archangel, and with the trump of God: and the dead in Christ shall rise first: then we which are alive and remain shall be caught up together with them in the clouds, to meet the Lord in the air: and so shall we ever be with the Lord.*

There are four points in each statement; they cover one another exactly and make it clear that Paul's words are an inspired commentary on our Lord's words. Jesus says, *I will come again.*

Paul says, *The Lord himself shall descend from heaven with a shout, with the voice of the archangel, and with the trump of God.*

Jesus says, *I will . . . receive you unto myself.*

Paul says, *We . . . shall be caught up together with them in the clouds, to meet the Lord in the air.*

Jesus says, *That where I am, there ye may be also.*

Paul says, *So shall we ever be with the Lord.*

Jesus says in introducing this promise, *Let not your heart be troubled.*

Paul says in closing, *Wherefore comfort one another with these words.*

Take Matthew 13:33: *The kingdom of heaven is like unto leaven, which a woman took, and hid in three measures of meal, till the whole was leavened.* Now some say this means that the kingdom of God, the truth of God, and the gospel of God are going to gradually grow and spread until they pervade the whole world. Others say that the leaven represents the corrupt doctrine that the woman, an apostate church, mixes in the children's bread and which multiplies like the yeast germs until the whole life and doctrine of the church is leavened. Which is right? Turn to 1 Corinthians 5:6-8, and you get God's answer to this important question: *Know ye not that a little leaven leaveneth the whole lump? Purge out therefore the old leaven, that ye may be a new lump, as ye are unleavened. For even Christ our passover is sacrificed for us: therefore let us keep the feast, not with old leaven, neither with the leaven of malice and wickedness; but with the unleavened bread of sincerity and truth.*

This is an inspired commentary on our Lord's words

and makes it as clear as day that the leaven refers to corruption, error, and sin.

The Bible itself is the very best commentary on the Bible. There is not a doubtful or difficult passage in the Bible anywhere that some other passage does not clear up and explain if we seek long enough for it. The best book to help you in finding these other passages that clear up uncertainties and solve difficulties is *The Treasury of Scripture Knowledge*. Of several possible explanations of a passage, choose the one in harmony with the general teaching or trend of the Bible. If anyone received a letter from me that had a statement in it that was capable of two interpretations, one of which was in harmony with the general tenor of my letter and my other writings, and one of which was utterly in conflict with the general trend of my letter and my other writings, he would not hesitate for one moment to give the interpretation that was in harmony with the general teaching and trend of my letter and of my other writings. So we ought to do likewise in interpreting the Bible. This does not mean that we are to distort and twist a passage out of its obvious meaning, so there may be no apparent contradiction between it and some other clear passage in the Bible.

One of the most vicious principles of Bible interpretation is that we must reconcile every passage with the teaching of every other passage. As the Bible is the revelation of an infinite mind that presents all sides of the truth, it is inevitable that there would be in it two lines of truth which may be perfectly easy to reconcile in a mind of infinite wisdom, but which we in our limitations of thought and one-sidedness of thought cannot reconcile at all. For example, we are not to try to explain away the clear teaching of the Word of God as to the sovereignty of God on the one hand, or the clear teaching of the Word of God as to the freedom of the human will on the other hand. But if there are several easily possible interpretations of a passage and one fits more harmoniously with the general teaching and trend of the Bible than the other, that is the one to be accepted.

Interpret Obscure Passages in the Light of Passages That Are Perfectly Plain

The tenth principle of correct biblical interpretation is to interpret obscure passages in the light of passages that are perfectly plain. Many do just the opposite. There will be a number of passages whose meanings are as plain as day. There will be another passage which is more or less obscure, and people will ignore all these perfectly plain passages and try to explain them away in the uncertain light of the obscure passage. The other procedure, comparing with a plain text, would be the rational one.

Take, for example, 1 Corinthians 9:27: *I keep under my body, and bring it into subjection: lest that by any means, when I have preached to others, I myself should be a castaway* – or rather, be disapproved. Now this might seem to imply a fear on Paul's part that, even after his faithful work, he might be lost. However, taking the exact force of the words and looking up their biblical usage, we find that the verse is much more practical than this – Paul is simply making it clear why he keeps his body in subjection, and also makes this statement as a warning to others who may think they can have faith without obedience.

He says in 2 Timothy 1:12, *For the which cause I also suffer these things: nevertheless I am not ashamed: for I know whom I have believed, and am persuaded that he is able to keep that which I have committed unto him against that day.*

And he says in 2 Timothy 4:18, *The Lord shall deliver me from every evil work, and will preserve me unto his heavenly kingdom: to whom be the glory for ever and ever.*

And our Lord Jesus Christ distinctly said in John 10:28, *I give unto them eternal life; and they shall never perish, neither shall any man pluck them out of my hand.*

And in 1 John 2:19, John says, *They went out from us, but they were not of us; for if they had been of us, they would no doubt have continued with us: but they went out, that they might be made manifest that they were not all of us,* thus distinctly teaching that when one is really born again, he will not fall away.

Interpret Any Passage As Those Who Were Addressed

The eleventh principle of correct biblical interpretation is to interpret any passage in the Bible as those who were addressed would have understood it. Words that were addressed to any people were intended to be understood by them. There may be exceptions to this principle, but they are rare. An illustration of an exception is found in John 2:19, where Jesus says, *Destroy this temple, and in three days I will raise it up.* John tells us Jesus was speaking of the temple of His body, but the Jews would not have understood that. In this case our Lord Jesus was not speaking for the present moment but for the days that were to come. John explains this when he says, *When therefore he was risen from the dead, his disciples remembered that he had said this unto them; and they believed the scripture, and the word which Jesus had said* (John 2:22).

In interpreting the Bible, we need to have a knowledge of the times and places and customs where the words were spoken. For example, our Lord said to Peter in Matthew 16:19, *I will give unto thee the keys of the kingdom of heaven: and whatsoever thou shalt bind on earth shall be bound in heaven: and whatsoever thou shalt loose on earth shall be loosed in heaven.* Now this was perfectly understood by those to whom he said it, because they knew the customs of the day. When one graduated from one of the rabbinical classes, he was given by the rabbi a "key" to indicate that he was now ready to open the secrets of the kingdom. So our Lord promised to Peter *the keys of the kingdom of heaven* to indicate that Peter would be able to open the truth of the kingdom of heaven to men. We see Peter using the keys with the Jews on the day of Pentecost and with the gentiles in the household of Cornelius. There was another well-known usage of the day that explains the remainder of the verse. The words *bind* and *loose* were used constantly by the rabbis as referring to "forbidding" and "permitting." For example, Shammai, a very strict rabbi, was said to bind, or forbid, what Hillel, a more generous and liberal rabbi, was said to loose, or permit.

Interpret According to the Proper Audience

The twelfth principle of correct biblical interpretation is to interpret what belongs to the Christian as belonging to the Christian, what belongs to the Jew as belonging to the Jew, and what belongs to the gentiles as belonging to the gentiles. One of the most common causes of misinterpretation of the Bible is taking what is said or what applies to one group of people and applying it to another group. Take, for example, Romans 8:35: *Who shall separate us from the love of Christ? shall tribulation, or distress, or persecution, or famine, or nakedness, or peril, or sword?* Now this is distinctly said, as the context clearly shows, to the believer, the one who is foreordained, called, and justified. Many take it as teaching that nothing can separate anybody from the love of Christ. It teaches nothing of the kind.

Interpret Each Writer with a View to the Opinions the Writer Opposed

The thirteenth principle of correct biblical interpretation is to interpret each writer with a view to the opinions the writer opposed. That is to say, when interpreting Paul as he is opposing the Judaizing tendencies in certain circles of his day, we should bear that in mind as we interpret his epistles, such as the epistle to the Romans and the epistle to the Galatians. When we are interpreting James, we should bear in mind that he was opposing the antinomians of his day who taught that if a man believed correctly about Christ, he was under no moral obligations; he could live as he pleased and still be a saved man. In interpreting John in his first epistle, we should bear in mind that he was opposing the Gnostics of his day who were degrading Christianity by combining it with a fantastic philosophy similar to the philosophy of Christian Science, and in some forms of Gnosticism combining it with the philosophy of Theosophy.

Interpret Poetry As Poetry and Prose As Prose

The fourteenth principle of correct biblical interpretation is to interpret poetry as poetry and prose as prose. For example, in interpreting Psalm 18, we should bear in mind that it is highly poetic, a remarkably vivid, poetic description of a thunderstorm in which God put forth His power in defense of His servant. The highly poetic character of the psalm should be kept in mind in interpreting the psalm; for example, the eighth verse says, *There went up a smoke out of his nostrils, and fire out of his mouth devoured: coals were kindled by it.* Now this is not to be taken literally as representing God as a Being out of whose nose poured literal smoke and out of whose mouth poured literal fire. It is a wonderfully vivid and highly poetic description of a thunderstorm. Some people have no poetic sense and do everything in a matter-of-fact way.

The story is told of a man of this hopelessly prosaic type of mind who read the well-known verse, "There are books in brooks, sermons in stones, and good in everything,"[5] and he at once made this criticism: "That is not what the writer meant to say. What he meant to say was that there are sermons in books, stones in brooks, and good in everything." Poetry should be interpreted as poetry. That is not to say it does not mean what it says, but it says it in a figurative way and sometimes in a vividly pictorial way that represents an idea by a picture.

But while we interpret poetry as poetry, we should interpret prose as prose. It is just as grave a breach of every sensible law of interpretation to interpret prose as poetry as it is to interpret poetry as prose. This is one of the outstanding faults of many of the "modern" interpreters of the Bible. They find a statement in the Bible that is evidently prose, but it contains a truth

---

5   William Shakespeare, *As You Like It*, 1603.

they do not wish to accept, so they at once say, "This is figurative." They criticize those "stupid" people who interpret poetry as prose but do not realize they are open to just as grave a criticism for interpreting prose as poetry.

The Holy Spirit Is the Best Interpreter of the Bible

The fifteenth principle of correct biblical interpretation is that the Holy Spirit is the best interpreter of the Bible. The best interpreter of any book is the author of the book, and the Holy Spirit is beyond any honest question the Author of the Bible. *For the prophecy came not in old time by the will of man: but holy men of God spake as they were moved* [more literally, being "borne along" or "carried along"] *by the Holy Spirit* (2 Peter 1:21). Since this is true, of course it admits that the Holy Spirit is the best interpreter of the Bible. The man who in his study of the Word seeks and obtains the illumination of the Holy Spirit is a far more dependable interpreter of the Word than the greatest scholar on earth who is not illumined by the Holy Spirit.

As we pointed out before, *the natural man receiveth not the things of the Spirit of God: for they are foolishness unto him: neither can he know them, because they are spiritually discerned* (1 Corinthians 2:14). Therefore, no matter how well founded one's claims to scholarship may be, if he is not a Spirit-taught man, his interpretations of the Word of God are absolutely valueless. The humblest and most uneducated Christian here who is taught by the Spirit of God would be a far more competent and reliable interpreter of the Scripture than the greatest university professor or theological professor on earth who was not in right relationship with God and, therefore, was not taught by the Spirit of God.

Our Lord Jesus said to His disciples on the night before His crucifixion, *Howbeit when he, the Spirit of truth, is come, he will guide you into all truth* (John 16:13). Now while this promise was made primarily to the apostles, and is a guarantee of their inspiration and their absolute dependability as teachers, it also belongs in a lesser way to the individual believer. John, the beloved disciple, applies it to the believer. He says in 1 John 2:27, *But the anointing [the Holy Spirit] which ye have received of him [from Christ] abideth in you, and ye need not that any man teach you: but as the same anointing teacheth you of all things.*

So in your study of the Bible, in your eager desire to discover its true meaning, in your determination to find out the exact mind of God as He has revealed it in His Word, above all else seek the guidance of the

86

Holy Spirit. The way to get His guidance is to ask for it. Our Lord Jesus said, *If ye then, being evil, know how to give good gifts unto your children: how much more shall your heavenly Father give the Holy Spirit to them that ask him?* (Luke 11:13).

How often have you thought as you have heard some Bible teacher who has been especially helpful to you, "Oh, if I could only go to that man every day and have him for my teacher, I would make some progress in the knowledge of the things of God!" But every time you open your Bible by yourself, you can have a far more competent and skillful teacher than any human Bible teacher this world ever saw. You will have the Author of the Book to interpret it to you, and the greatest of all secrets of true interpretation of the Word of God is to have the Spirit of God for your interpreter of the Word. And if you are in right relationship with God, trusting in the finished work of Jesus Christ as the sole ground of your acceptance before God, looking to the risen Christ to give you daily victory over sin, and if you are absolutely surrendered in your will and your affections and your thoughts to the will and mind of God, and then ask the Holy Spirit each time you open the Word to come and interpret it to you, then you may have the Holy Spirit as your interpreter every time you open the Book.

Chapter 4

The Seven Great Promises of God...

...for the Bible Student and Soul Winner

I have turned over the matter in my mind for some weeks as to what subject I should speak on this morning to the graduating class. I thought it was settled in my mind that I should speak on 2 Timothy 4:5: *Make full proof of thy ministry.* But not many days ago, I was so stirred by reading a book entitled *Modern Religious Liberalism* that I was strongly disposed to speak on "What to Do with the Bible," and had the sermon outlined in my mind. But when I went to God in definite prayer about it last Monday afternoon, He gave me this subject: "The Seven Great Promises of God for the Bible Student and Soul Winner."

For two years you have been diligently studying the Bible under the direction and encouragement of some of the best-known students and teachers of the Bible in the world. You have been studying it not merely so that you might get as complete an intellectual mastery of it as possible, but also so that you might find equipment for the most glorious work in the world – soul winning. But you certainly are not foolish enough to think that your studies are now at an end. Only a hopeless fool could imagine for a moment that two years of study anywhere, or under any teachers that ever lived, could exhaust this Book in which are hidden the infinite and inexhaustible treasures of the wisdom and knowledge of God. Your Bible studies are just beginning.

Bible study is to be your lifelong employment, and you are going out to wear yourselves out in the great work for which you have been preparing – soul winning. You will not all be foreign missionaries or ministers of the gospel at home, but you are to be soul winners all your days. Some of you will be in the foreign field, some in large churches, some in small churches, some in obscure and neglected unchurched fields at home, and some of you in that most hallowed of all fields of soul winning upon which the Bible lays so much emphasis – the Christian home. But all of you, by the good hand of God, are to be soul winners. I can think of no more appropriate subject for this most joyous, and at the same time most solemn, occasion than that which I have announced: "The Seven Great Promises of God for the Bible Student and Soul Winner."

The First Great Promise

The first great promise is from Psalm 1:1-3: *Blessed is the man that walketh not in the counsel of the ungodly, nor standeth in the way of sinners, nor sitteth in the seat of the scornful. But his delight is in the law of the* LORD; *and in his law doth he meditate day and night. And he shall be like a tree planted by the rivers of water, that bringeth forth his fruit in his season; his leaf also shall not wither; and whatsoever he doeth shall prosper.*

Please look again at that promise steadily and with open eyes and clear eyes until you take in its wonderful meaning: *Blessed is the man that walketh not in the counsel of the ungodly, nor standeth in the way of sinners, nor sitteth in the seat of the scornful. But his delight is in the law of the* LORD; *and in his law doth he meditate day and night. And he shall be like a tree planted by the rivers of water, that bringeth forth his fruit in his season; his leaf also shall not wither; and whatsoever he doeth shall prosper.*

God promises the Bible student and the would-be soul winner that if he meets one of the fundamental conditions of profitable Bible study – thorough separation from the world – he will be fruitful. He must not walk in the counsel of the ungodly, stand in the way of sinners, or sit in the seat of the scornful, but must meditate on God's law, the revealed will of God as found in this Book, which is the Word of God (Mark 7:13; 1 Thessalonians 2:13). If he meditates on it day and night, then he shall be a fruitful tree, a constantly, perpetually fruitful tree, a well-watered tree, watered by the streams of life that flow from the throne of God through the channels of this wonderful Book. *And whatsoever he doeth shall prosper.* What an amazing promise! What a stupendous promise! And what an all-sufficient promise for the Bible student who is about to enter his lifework. Young men and women, you certainly long for a good share of prosperity. But oh, think of it; there is a way to make sure that everything you might do in these coming days and years shall prosper. If anyone in your position can face a promise like that and not have to put forth some effort to keep from shouting, I can hardly understand it.

Be Sure You Meet the Conditions of the Promise
The first condition is separation from the world in all your conduct, not walking *in the counsel* or advice of those who are not fully surrendered to God, not standing *in the way* that sinners go, or sitting down *in the*

seat of the scornful or scoffers. This includes all "higher critics" and "new theology" men and other infidels, whose chief stock-in-trade is making light of what God Himself says and of the most fundamental and precious doctrines of our faith. If you find yourself located in some seat of learning where, as at the University of Chicago, they make light of the precious truths of God (that is, *scornful* ones in the Authorized Version and *scoffers* in the Revised Standard Version), leave that *seat* immediately; do not sit *in the seat of scoffers.*

The second condition is that you meditate on God's Word day and night, that is, that you deeply, profoundly, continuously ponder the revelation God has made in this Book, and that you not merely study the Bible for a quarter of an hour or a half hour or even an hour every day, but that you also store up in your mind and heart what you discover, and ponder it day and night. Young men and women, never forget that. A great pressure of work will be on you in the coming days, and many books, papers, magazines, and reviews will clamor for your attention. Stoutly and steadfastly refuse to let the demands of service or of other literature crowd out the precious Word of God, upon which meditation day and night spells prosperity in everything you undertake.

Why is it that so many missionaries and ministers

and other Christian workers prosper so little? The answer is found right here: they give so little time to actually meditating upon the Word of God, and they let work or other lines of study crowd out the Word of God, or they ponder it without that clearness of vision that comes from clear-cut separation from the world and from all modernists and other scoffers.

The Second Great Promise

The second great promise of God for the Bible student and soul winner is Daniel 12:3: *And they that be wise shall shine as the brightness of the firmament; and they that turn many to righteousness as the stars for ever and ever.* This is a great promise for Bible students as well as for soul winners, for only the Bible student is really *wise.* It is *the entrance of [God's] words [that] giveth light; [that] giveth understanding unto the simple* (Psalm 119:130). No one can be truly wise, wise with real wisdom, the wisdom that counts for eternity as well as time, unless he is a Bible student. So God tells us in this striking promise that the Bible student *shall shine as the brightness of the firmament,* and the soul winner as *the stars for ever and ever.* Every red-blooded man and every woman who is worthwhile longs to shine. If you did not wish to shine for your own sake, you ought to have a great ambition to shine for our Lord Jesus Christ's sake. He Himself bids us to shine. He says in Matthew 5:14 and 16, *Ye are the light of the world. . . . Let your light so shine before men, that they may see your good works, and glorify your Father which is in heaven.* This promise tells us how to shine, how to gloriously shine; how to shine not for the few brief days of this fleeting life that now is, but forever and ever. Be a Bible student, a real Bible student, and be a soul winner; for *they that be wise shall shine as the brightness of the firmament; and they that turn many to righteousness as the stars for ever and ever.*

Oh, that large but foolish company of men and women, including not a few ministers and theological teachers and writers, desires to shine down here and have a cheap reputation for advanced scholarship. They forget that the history of the world and the church is forever demonstrating that the advanced scholarship of today is the ridiculous nonsense of tomorrow. Young men and women, listen; it is not worthwhile to shine down here and get all sorts of degrees and titles attached to your name if you are untrue to God and His inspired Word. Look back and see how the shores of past time are strewn with the whitened wrecks of men who shone in an apostate church. No, don't care a fig to shine as a great pulpit orator, pulpit humorist, pulpit swindler, or pulpit comforter by holding out false hopes to those who desire to live careless, worldly, and pleasure-seeking lives. It does not pay to shine down here, even as a golden-tongued pulpit orator. It does pay to shine up yonder, to shine *as the stars for ever and ever.* And there is only one way to shine up yonder – by being a real Bible student and soul winner.

The Third Great Promise

The third great promise of God for the Bible student and soul winner you will find in Psalm 126:6: *He that goeth forth and weepeth, bearing precious seed, shall doubtless come again with rejoicing, bringing his sheaves with him.* Here is another promise that stirs the alert and intelligent soul to its very depths. What intelligent harvester does not long to come home laden down with mighty sheaves of golden grain? But what other harvest is so desirable as the harvest of precious souls? This, too, is a promise, as we shall see shortly, for both the Bible student and soul winner, a soul winner just because he is a Bible student. It tells us how to come, when our brief but laborious harvest time is over, bringing our golden sheaves with us. *He that goeth forth and weepeth, bearing precious seed, shall doubtless come again with rejoicing, bringing his sheaves with him.* There are just three conditions of a bountiful harvest: *goeth forth, weepeth,* and *bearing precious seed.* Let me change the order.

First, *bearing precious seed.* Our Lord Jesus tells us in Luke 8:11 what the *precious seed* is that must be borne if we are to reap an abundant harvest of the right sort: *The seed is the word of God.* That is the only seed that is worth sowing or that will bring a harvest of souls. Men are born again, Peter tells us, *not of corruptible seed, but of incorruptible, by the word of God, which liveth and abideth for ever* (1 Peter 1:23). To sow the Word, we must know the Word; so you can see how this is a promise for the Bible student as well as for the soul winner. The Revised Standard Version reads *seed for sowing* in place of *precious seed.* The Hebrew words mean just that, or "a sowing of seed," and the only seed that is fit for sowing in the prepared soil of the human heart is God's Word.

Here, too, we see why it is that so many preachers, missionaries, and personal workers gather such scant harvests; they are sowing something beside the Word of God. Go listen to many sermons and note how little there is of the unmixed seed of the Word of God in them. You will hear much bull's-eye daisies, chess (*Bromus secalinus*), and Canadian thistles of man's notions, whims, speculations, and conceits. Their churches look like some alleged "wheat fields" that we see, full of daisies, mustard, devil's paintbrush, Canadian thistles, bull thistles, and nettles. Oh, young men and women, always bear the *precious seed* of God's Word and only that. If someone tells you it won't draw like poetry, moonshine, advanced thought, and movies, think of Moody and Spurgeon and some of the things your own eyes have seen these past months in this very building and elsewhere.

Then note the words *goeth forth. He that goeth forth and weepeth, bearing precious seed, shall doubtless come again with rejoicing, bringing his sheaves with him.* It is not enough to have the seed; go sow it. Sow it far and wide throughout America, not forgetting the neglected fields through China, Japan, Africa, India, and everywhere. It is not the seed the farmer has in his granary that brings a harvest, but the seed he sows in his field; and it is not the truth you know, but the truth you sow that will bear a harvest. Remember it is *seed for sowing*, and the truth you have learned from the study of God's Word and the truth you shall learn in your future study of the Word is *seed for sowing.* Never forget that. Many a man who knows little gathers a more abundant harvest than many who know much, for what little he knows he diligently sows.

And in regard to this promise, note the words *and*

weepeth. It is not enough to know the Word of God, and it is not enough to sow the Word of God. If you desire a bounteous harvest, you must water the seed with your tears as you sow. Experience also abundantly proves that the Word of God that is given with a heart full of love for sinners, a love that shows itself in tears of sympathy for the sinner's sorrows, and tears of pain over the sinner's sin and stubbornness, is what bears fruit in souls saved. Here is where many missionaries in the foreign field fail, and many preachers at home fail; they have no deep, heartfelt love that leads to tears for those to whom they preach and with whom they work.

One of the mightiest soul winners among the outcast that this country ever saw was Colonel George Clark, the founder of the Pacific Garden Mission in Chicago. Colonel Clark worked faithfully at his business six days of the week so he could preach the gospel without pay seven nights in the week. Every night they would gather at the Pacific Garden Mission, four or five hundred men, mostly of the down-and-out class. They would hang on every word Colonel Clark spoke, though he was not an interesting speaker; indeed, he was a very ordinary and commonplace speaker. I never heard him give an original thought in all my life, and yet those outcasts would sit all evening and hang on his words. Some of the most brilliant speakers in America would go there and could not hold that crowd, but Colonel Clark always could.

I studied these strange phenomena and finally found the explanation for them. They knew that Colonel Clark loved them, that he would give his last penny for them, that he would wear his life out for them, as he actually did. Colonel Clark was a man given to tears as he spoke. He was a large, powerful man, weighing perhaps 250 pounds, and tears from such a man seemed out of place; after a while he became ashamed of his many tears and held them back. But he found that with the drying-up of his tears, he lost his power. He went to God and cried, "Oh, God, give me back my tears," and God gave him back his tears and gave him back his power.

Young men and women, cultivate a real, heartfelt love for those among whom you work. Ask the Holy Spirit to make their lost condition real to you and to make their coming doom vivid to you if they are not saved. It is not the one who knows the most but the one who loves the most who wins the most. I think I would make a good missionary to the Chinese, for I love the Chinese; I confess I love them more than I do any other people. But look to God to give you a tear-bringing love for any people among whom you work.

The Fourth Great Promise

The fourth great promise of God for the Bible student and soul winner you will find in James 1:5: *If any of you lack wisdom, let him ask of God, that giveth to all men liberally, and upbraideth not; and it shall be given him.* This, too, is a great promise for the Bible student and soul winner. To be a successful student of the Word, one needs wisdom, and to be a successful soul winner, one needs great wisdom and tact. This promise tells how to get this wisdom – ask for it. *If any of you lack wisdom, let him ask of God, that giveth to all men liberally, and upbraideth not; and it shall be given him.* What to do is in one word: *ask* – definite, believing prayer. The next two verses say, Our promise tells us very clearly of whom to ask. It is put in two words: *of God.* Be very clear about that. There is much asking that is not really *of God.* Men pray, but they do not really get into the presence of God and ask *of Him.* Be sure you enter His presence every time you pray.

And note carefully of which God to ask – the *God, that giveth to all men liberally, and upbraideth not.* Only one God does that, the God and Father of our Lord and Savior, Jesus Christ. There is much that is called praying today that is not unto Him.

Professor Theodore Gerald Soares, professor of

Homiletics and Religious Education and head of the Department of Practical Theology at the University of Chicago, says, "The mental state of peace, exultation, and resolution which issue upon the exercise of prayer are due to the release of conscious tension." But that certainly is not praying to the *God, that giveth to all men liberally, and upbraideth not,* even if the writer is a theological professor.

President G. Stanley Hall of Clark University, Worcester, Massachusetts, says that prayer is "communion with the deeper racial self within us." But that certainly is not asking of the *God, that giveth to all men liberally, and upbraideth not.*

Professor George Burman Foster, who was a professor in the theological department at the University of Chicago and then professor of Philosophy of Religion in another department in the university until the time of his death, said, "The only prayer which we have a moral right to pray is precisely the prayer which after all we ourselves must answer." But that certainly is not asking of the *God, that giveth to all men liberally, and upbraideth not.*

Professor Edward Scribner Ames, associate professor of the University of Chicago and pastor of Hyde Park Church of Disciples of Christ, in his book *The New Orthodoxy,* says, "For the modern man standing erect in his pride of power, the old ceremony full of passivity and surrender is a symbol of a dying age." But that certainly is not asking of the *God, that giveth to all men liberally, and upbraideth not.*

Professor Gerald Birney Smith, professor of Christian Theology at the University of Chicago, says, "The worship of God in a democracy will consist in reverence for those human values which democracy makes supreme." But that certainly is not asking of the *God, that giveth to all men liberally, and upbraideth not.* I would rather send a son of mine to a smallpox hospital as a health resort than send him to a theological seminary or university where such blasphemous folly as that is taught as a preparation for an efficient ministry or for missionary work. Have our Baptists, Methodists, and Presbyterians gone mad that they send their children to institutions where such wicked, blasphemous, and practically atheistic things are taught? Real prayer to a real God, the only true God, the God and Father of our Lord and Savior Jesus Christ, brings wondrous wisdom in the study of the Word of God and in soul winning. No other shovel digs so deeply into the gold mine of God's Word and throws out such nuggets of pure gold as prayer, real prayer to a real God. No other rainmaker will so operate upon the clouds of God's abundant grace that always hang over us and bring down such mighty outpourings of the Holy Spirit manifesting themselves in a multitude of souls won as real prayer to a real God. Never forget that. Never, never, never.

The Fifth Great Promise

This naturally and inevitably brings us to the fifth great promise of God for the Bible student and soul winner. You will find it in Acts 1:8: *Ye shall receive power, after that the Holy Spirit is come upon you: and ye shall be witnesses unto me both in Jerusalem, and in all Judaea, and in Samaria, and unto the uttermost part of the earth.* The great need of missionary, minister, personal worker, father, and mother when they study God's Word and when they go out to win souls is power. They need power to penetrate the sacred cloisters of God's Word where such abundant treasures of truth are stored, and power to present to others the truth discovered in such a way as to convict of sin and reveal Jesus Christ to bring men to accept Jesus as their Lord and Savior and thus be born again. This verse reveals the great secret of that power: *Ye shall receive power, after that the Holy Spirit is come upon you: and ye shall be witnesses unto me both in Jerusalem, and in all Judaea, and in Samaria, and unto the uttermost part of the earth.* We need a power not from this earth, not from human culture, not the power learned in schools of oratory, or the power that comes from the tricks of the world, baptized with Christian names as in the Interchurch World Movement. We need power, but not the power to draw crowds learned from Douglas Fairbanks, Mary Pickford, or Charlie Chaplin, crystallized in the introduction of the movies into the Sunday evening service, turning the sacred house of God into a third-class Sunday theatrical performance. No! No! No!

Power from on high (Luke 24:49); this promise in Acts 1:8 tells us how to get it. It tells us how any graduate of the Bible Institute or any child of God can get it. Listen again: *Ye shall receive power, after that the Holy Spirit is come upon you: and ye shall be witnesses unto me both in Jerusalem, and in all Judaea, and in Samaria, and unto the uttermost part of the earth.* This is the definite baptism with the Holy Spirit of which Peter spoke on the day of Pentecost immediately after he had been *baptized with the Holy Spirit* (Acts 1:5). *For the promise is unto you, and to your children, and to all that are afar off, even as many as the Lord our God shall call* (Acts 2:39).

The Sixth Great Promise

This then leads us directly to the sixth great promise

of God for the Bible student and soul winner. You will find it in Luke 11:13: *If ye then, being evil, know how to give good gifts unto your children: how much more shall your heavenly Father give the Holy Spirit to them that ask him?* The fifth promise tells us that *power from on high,* power right from God, God's own power, will be upon us after the Holy Spirit comes upon us. The sixth promise tells us how to make sure of the Holy Spirit coming upon you: *If ye then, being evil, know how to give good gifts unto your children: how much more shall your heavenly Father give the Holy Spirit to them that ask him?* The way is very simple: just *ask,* ask Him; that is, ask God, the only true God, the heavenly Father, not the God that is immanent in humanity of which these wise "new theologians" boast. But ask the God and Father of our Lord and Savior Jesus Christ, who is in heaven, the real God, the God who actually is, and not the God of man's mad imaginings.

Professor Walter Rauschenbusch, now dead (died in 1918), formerly professor of Church History at Rochester Theological Seminary, a Baptist institution, said, "The old conception that God . . . is distinct from our human life" must give way to "the religious belief that He is immanent [indwelt] in humanity." Don't ask for the Holy Spirit of such a God as that; ask for the real God, your Father in heaven.

Professor Josiah Royce of Harvard University says, "The divine is no more separate and aloof. It is within and organic with the human." The same thought is elsewhere put in these words: "God is considered as the soul of the world, the spirit animating nature, the universal force which takes the myriad forms of heat, light, gravitation, electricity, and the like." Don't ask any such God as that to give you the Holy Spirit. You might as well pray to a Hindu or Chinese idol or an Alaskan totem.

Professor Gerald Birney Smith, quoted earlier, speaks of God as "the spiritual forces of the world in which we live, the unseen forces of the universe." Don't ask that God for the Holy Spirit.

Professor Royce defines God as the immanent "spirit of the community." Don't ask that God for the Holy Spirit. No, don't pray to the God of any of this type of theological seminary and university professors who, *professing themselves to be wise, . . . [have become] fools* (Romans 1:22). Pray to the real God, the God whom the Lord Jesus revealed in His words and in His person, our heavenly Father, the God who really is and really answers prayer. And if you are His child, He will answer, and He will baptize you and fill you with His Holy Spirit. You will have power, and no man will be *able to resist the wisdom and the spirit by which he spake* (Acts 6:10).

The Seventh Great Promise

Now we come to the seventh and last great promise of God for the Bible student and soul winner, and in some respects, it is the best of all. It is the direct outcome of the sixth promise and closely related to the fifth and fourth promises. You will find it in Matthew 28:19-20: *Go ye therefore, and teach all nations, baptizing them in the name of the Father, and of the Son, and of the Holy Spirit: teaching them to observe all things whatsoever I have commanded you: and, lo, I am with you alway, even unto the end of the world.*

Oh, what a promise! The promise of the personal presence of our Lord Jesus Himself with us all the time until the consummation of the age, when He will come visibly and bodily to take us to be with Him forever. He is now our unseen Lord (1 Peter 1:8) up in glory, interceding for us (Hebrews 7:25), taking up our case, and advocating it and carrying it through.

But He is also our present Lord. It is the work of the Holy Spirit, when He comes to us, to form within us an indwelling Christ. The Lord Jesus Himself said to His disciples the night before He left them:

*If ye love me, keep my commandments. And
I will pray the Father, and he shall give you
another Comforter, that he may abide with
you for ever; even the Spirit of truth; whom
the world cannot receive, because it seeth him
not, neither knoweth him: but ye know him;
for he dwelleth with you, and shall be in you.
I will not leave you comfortless: I will come to
you. Yet a little while, and the world seeth me
no more; but ye see me: because I live, ye shall
live also. At that day ye shall know that I am
in my Father, and ye in me, and I in you. He
that hath my commandments, and keepeth
them, he it is that loveth me: and he that
loveth me shall be loved of my Father, and
I will love him, and will manifest myself to
him. Judas saith unto him, not Iscariot, Lord,
how is it that thou wilt manifest thyself unto
us, and not unto the world? Jesus answered
and said unto him, If a man love me, he will
keep my words: and my Father will love him,
and we will come unto him, and make our
abode with him.* (John 14:15-23)

Yes, He is really with us, not visibly as in that glad

coming day; He will be, nonetheless, really and consciously with us.

Young men and women, as you leave these halls and these friendships with the faculty and your fellow students that have become so precious to you, you will have many lonely hours and lonely days and lonely weeks. I think the loneliest day I ever saw up to that time was the day I graduated at Yale and left the city on a late boat for New York. Most of my class took earlier trains. It seemed as if I would almost die of loneliness. Forty-six years have passed, but the memory of the misery of that night lingers with me still. And you will have lonely days. And when you get into the heart of China and into the heart of Africa and into Indian jungles, you will see lonely days. But you need not see lonely days; you need not see a lonely hour or a lonely minute. By day and by night, you may have the dearest and best and most satisfying of all companions, our glorious Lord Jesus Himself. Listen again to this crowning promise of all: *Go ye therefore, and teach all nations, baptizing them in the name of the Father, and of the Son, and of the Holy Spirit: teaching them to observe all things whatsoever I have commanded you: and, lo, I am with you alway, even unto the end of the world.*

Ah, this coming summer when some night I am up alone on the Yangtze River or elsewhere, out in some lonely mountain or desert plain, I could be lonely, but I won't be. Jesus will be there, and He will be with you too if you meet the conditions.

Note these conditions well: *Go ye therefore, and teach all nations, baptizing them in the name of the Father, and of the Son, and of the Holy Spirit: teaching them to observe all things whatsoever I have commanded you: and, lo, I am with you alway, even unto the end of the world.*

If you go out into all the world making disciples, going as far as your line may extend, be it eighteen miles or eighteen thousand miles, He will go with you. But if you do not listen sharply for His call and go as far as He bids you to go, He will not go with you. If we go His way, He will go ours, but if we do not go His way, He will not go ours. If God says Africa, and your foolish heart says southern California, He will not go with you. Amid the dearest friends on earth, you will be supremely lonely. But if you say with Isaiah when the Lord Jesus calls – and He is calling now – *Here am I; send me* (Isaiah 6:8), He will send you, and He will go along. You may be alone beneath the silent stars on some African tableland, but you will not be alone. He, our glorious Lord, will walk by your side. And He is enough. And you will walk with Him forever, for He has said, *If any man serve me, let him follow me; and where I am, there shall also my servant be: if any man serve me, him will my Father honour* (John 12:26).

Young men and women of the graduating class, you have been here at the Bible Institute of Los Angeles for two years. You have worked hard. You have done well. You have made satisfactory progress in your study of the Word of God, in your Christian character, and in your work for Christ. You have won the confidence, respect, and love of every member of the faculty, and I think we can rest confident that we have won your love as well as your confidence. You are about to leave us; we are sorry to have you go, for we shall greatly miss you.

When I come back next November and look out over the seats in the lecture room, my first impulse will be to look for the faces that I know so well and to listen for the voices that I have learned to distinguish from one another. I shall miss you, and every member of the faculty will miss you. But we are glad you are going. There was never in all this world's history such a crying demand for men and women who know God, who know Jesus Christ, filled with the Holy Spirit, and who know their Bibles and how to use them in winning souls for Christ, as in the day in which you and I live. We shall follow you with our prayers. We expect you to do credit to the institute that sends you both by your holy living and your effective service, but what is infinitely more important, to do credit to our God and Father and to our Lord and Savior Jesus Christ. God bless you.

The End

Reuben A. Torrey – A Brief Biography

R euben A. Torrey was an author, conference
speaker, pastor, evangelist, Bible college dean,
and more. Reuben Archer Torrey was born in Hoboken,
New Jersey, on January 28, 1856. He graduated from
Yale University in 1875 and from Yale Divinity School
in 1878, when he became the pastor of a Congregational
church in Garrettsville, Ohio. Torrey married Clara
Smith in 1879, with whom he had five children.

In 1882, he went to Germany, where he studied at the

universities at Leipsic and Erlangen. Upon returning to the United States, R. A. Torrey pastored in Minneapolis, as well as being in charge of the Congregational City Mission Society. In 1889, D. L. Moody called upon Torrey to lead his Chicago Evangelization Society, which later became the Moody Bible Institute. Beginning in 1894, Torrey was also the pastor of the Chicago Avenue Church, which was later called the Moody Memorial Church. He was a chaplain with the YMCA during the Spanish-American War, and was also a chaplain during World War I.

Torrey traveled all over the world leading evangelistic tours, preaching to the unsaved. It is believed that more than 100,000 were saved under his preaching. In 1908, he helped start the Montrose Bible Conference in Pennsylvania, which continues today. He became dean of the Los Angeles Bible Institute (now BIOLA) in 1912, and was the pastor of the Church of the Open Door in Los Angeles from 1915-1924.

Torrey continued speaking all over the world and holding Bible conferences. He died in Asheville, North Carolina, on October 26, 1928.

R. A. Torrey was a very active evangelist and soul winner, speaking to people everywhere he went, in public and in private, about their souls, seeking to lead the lost to Jesus. He authored more than forty books, including *How to Bring Men to Christ*, *How to Pray*, *How to Study the Bible*, *How to Obtain Fullness of Power*, and *Why God Used D. L. Moody*, as well as editing the twelve-volume book about the fundamentals of the faith, titled *The Fundamentals*. He was also known as a man of prayer, and his teaching, preaching, writing, and his entire life proved that he walked closely with God.